THE
Living
World

Oxford University Press

Oxford University Press, Walton Street, Oxford *OX2 6DP*

Oxford   New York   Toronto
Delhi   Bombay   Calcutta   Madras   Karachi
Kuala Lumpur   Singapore   Hong Kong   Tokyo
Nairobi   Dar es Salaam   Cape Town
Melbourne   Auckland   Madrid

and associated companies in
Berlin   Ibadan

Oxford is a trade mark of Oxford University Press

© Oxford University Press 1993

British Library Cataloguing in Publication Data
Data available

ISBN 0-19-910142-6

Designed by Richard Morris, Stonesfield Design

Printed and bound in Great Britain by
Butler & Tanner Ltd, Frome and London

Foreword

Open *The Living World* and begin to explore the fascinating world of animals and plants: their biology, behaviour and evolution. Organized by biological classification, it will help you to build up a picture of how living things are related to each other, and how humans fit into that picture.

High-quality text and artwork from the *Oxford Children's Encyclopedia* have been adapted, and expanded with much new material, to produce this easy-to-use reference guide to *The Living World*.

How to use *The Living World*

Like all reference books you can use *The Living World* in two different ways. Make time to sit and browse through it for pleasure, and you will soon find yourself engrossed in a subject you would never have thought to look up.

The Living World is organized into sections based on how living things are classified; so you will find all the mammals together, all the birds, all the animals without backbones, and so on.

On another occasion you will want to find out about a particular subject, with no time for browsing. Using the index is the quickest way to find out where something is.

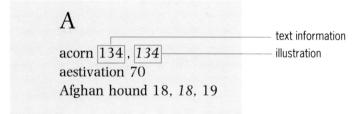

A

acorn 134 , *134* ————— text information
————— illustration
aestivation 70
Afghan hound 18, *18*, 19

Say you wanted to find out about acorn, you must turn to the index, which is always at the back of a book and organized alphabetically. Under the entry **acorn** you will find the same page number twice. The first number 134 tells you that you will be able to read about acorns by turning to page 134. The second number *134* in *italics*, tells you that you will also find a picture of an acorn on that page.

Contents

Foreword

Animals without backbones

Animal bodies at work

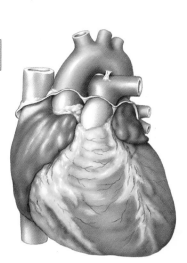

Plants

Evolution

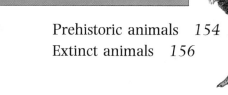

Acknowledgements

Illustrations & diagrams

Norman Arlott 4c, 48, 49, 50, 51, 52–53, 55, 56, 57, 63

Brian Beckett 5t, 13, 80, 81, 84, 88, 89, 92, 94, 102, 103, 126t, 127l

Jones Sewell Associates 111r

Frank Kennard 5c, 104, 105t, 106, 107, 108, 109, 110, 110–111, 112, 113, 116, 117, 118

Linden Artists

Graham Allen 36–37

Ray Hutchins 18–19

Gillian Kenny 5bl, 132, 138, 145, 198, 199

Mick Loates 4b, 72, 73, 75, 76–77, 78–79

David Moore 134, 134–135, 135, 136, 137

Oxford Illustrators Ltd 11, 126b, 127r

Andrew Robinson 5br, 148, 152, 153, 154–155, 156

Mike Saunders 66, 105b, 119, 120, 121, 122r, 124

Michael Woods title page, 4t, 7, 26, 27, 28, 29, 35, 37, 42, 44, 64, 65, 71, 78, 95, 98, 101, 122l, 122b, 123, 128, 129, 133, 139, 143, 144, 147

Photographs

Ace Photo Agency 14t, 15t, 26, 33t, 54b, 59br, 68t, 87

Andromeda Oxford 146

Heather Angel 17b, 21b, 24, 25t, 31t, 33b, 82bl, 130l

Brian Beckett 125r, 133tl tr & bc, 142 (tomato sequence tl tr & br)

Biofotos/Ian Took 74

Bruce Coleman 7l, 8, 9l & r, 10t & b, 11, 14b, 15b, 16t & b, 17, 18, 22, 23t, 27, 31b, 32t & b, 38t & b, 39, 41b, 42r, 43c, 45t, 46t & b, 47b, 53, 54t, 58b, 58–59t, 60, 61, 62l, 64, 65, 66t & b, 67t, 68b, 69t & b, 75, 79t, 82–83t, 86t & b, 88t, 90t & b, 91l & r, 92, 93b, 95, 96, 97t, 98, 100l, 100–101, 102, 103, 119, 130, 142 (bananas), 143, 145

Robert Harding Picture Library 137, 142 (pears)

International Centre for Conservation Education 71b (Mark Boulton)

Frank Lane Picture Agency 13, 28, 62r, 82cl, 118l

Richard Morris 142bl

National History Photographic Agency 7tr (George Bernard), 21t (Anthony Bannister), 23b (G Lacz), 40 (J Sauvanet), 42l (Stephen Dalton), 43bl (Anthony Bannister), 45br (H Palo), 47t (Stephen Dalton), 80 (Anthony Bannister), 97b (Bill Wood)

Oxford Scientific Films 12, 19, 20, 25b, 34, 41t, 43t, 44–45, 63, 67b, 70l, 70–71t, 76l, 82bcl, 82bcr, 82br, 83r, 85b, 99t, 101t, 118b, 120, 124, 125c, 131tr, 131b

Planet Earth Pictures 30, 35, 76–77b, 79

Joyce Pope 85t, 89

Science Photo Library 84, 93t, 99b, 108, 114–115, 125l, 149

Zefa 142 (3 photos plums, blackberries and cuckoopint)

Mammals

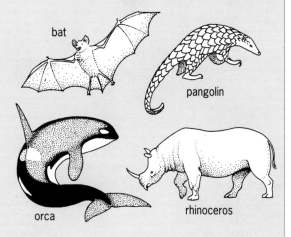

Mammals are the creatures that most of us mean when we say the word 'animals'. We know them best among all other living things, for many of our pets and domestic animals are mammals and so are we.

Mammals are found almost everywhere in the world, from the cold lands and seas of the Arctic to hot deserts and steamy forests, and there are many different kinds. Bats can fly; whales live only in water; moles are burrowers; antelopes and horses are runners; monkeys are climbers.

The first mammals were small and evolved at about the same time as the dinosaurs, 220 million years ago. When dinosaurs became extinct, mammals became the dominant land animals. Almost all large mammals are now under threat of extinction, mainly because of the activities of human beings.

Yellow baboon (left) and human (above) suckling. The name 'mammal' comes from the Latin word for breast, *mamma*, as all female mammals produce milk to feed their young.

Five things all mammals have in common.

1 All mammals have bones including a backbone.
2 All mammals have lungs and breathe dry air.
3 All mammals are warm-blooded.
4 All mammals have some fur or hair on their bodies.
5 All female mammals feed their babies on milk.

THREE GROUPS OF MAMMALS

The class Mammalia is divided into three groups depending on how the young develop.

The monotremes

A very small number of mammals hatch from eggs. They live only in Australia and New Guinea, and include the platypus.

platypus

The marsupials

The babies of these animals are minute at birth; some no larger than a grain of rice. In many species the tiny young crawl to a pouch on their mother's belly. There they feed on milk and grow in safety (not all marsupials have pouches). The marsupials are found mainly in Australia and New Guinea, but some also live in South and North America. Kangaroos and koalas are marsupials.

kangaroo

The placentals

The young are protected inside their mother's body for a long while before they are born. They are nourished through a special organ called the placenta which develops within the mother's body. Food and oxygen pass from her through the placenta to the young (embryo), and waste products are returned the same way. Most mammals are placentals.

bat

pangolin

orca

rhinoceros

Largest
Blue whale, up to 33 m in length and weighs 100–120 tonnes (heaviest recorded about 180 tonnes)

Smallest
Several species of shrew have a head and body length of less than 4·5 cm and weigh about 2 g. The hog-nosed bat of Thailand is about the same weight.

Longest lived
Generally large mammals live longer than small ones, but human beings live longer than most other mammals.

Apes

▶ Rwandan mountain gorillas grooming each other. Unusually it is the dominant male, the silverback, that is doing the grooming.

Distribution
Tropical rainforest in Central and West Africa (gorillas and chimpanzees), in Sumatra and Borneo (orang-utans), and in south-east Asia (gibbons).

Largest
Gorilla, up to 1·75 m tall, with an armspan of 2·75 m; weight up to 275 kg

Smallest
Gibbon, up to 65 cm tall; weight up to 6·7 kg

Number of young 1

Lifespan
About 40–50 years

Apes are our nearest relatives in the animal kingdom. There are two main groups of apes. Gibbons and siamangs are the lesser apes, and gorillas, chimpanzees and orangutans are the great apes. Like humans they are intelligent, long-lived animals, which generally travel in family parties. They have no visible tail; vision is their most important sense and, unlike most mammals, they can see colours much as we can.

There are many other similarities between apes and humans. Some of the blood proteins of chimpanzees are exactly the same as ours, and, as with humans, ape females normally have one baby at a time.

Young apes develop slowly. Ape mothers do not have another baby until the last one is several years old, by which time it is fairly independent. A baby chimpanzee, for example, is not weaned until it is about four years old. Until then it is cared for by

its mother, often riding on her back, and it will stay with her even after another birth.

Apes can climb very well and often swing about in the branches of trees, but adult great apes are too heavy for the higher, weaker branches. At night they construct nests out of branches to sleep in. They usually walk on all fours. This is known as knuckle walking, as they put their weight on their knuckles.

Much of the forests in which apes live has been destroyed. The orang-utan and the gorilla are both endangered species, and chimpanzees are much less common than they were.

Gorillas

Gorillas are the largest of the great apes. They are gentle creatures living in family groups led by a big male, the silverback. When they are old enough to breed, young females leave and join another group. Young males also leave, and may wander alone for years before forming a new group.

A gorilla's day starts at dawn (about 6 a.m.) when the party wakes and searches for food. From about 10 a.m. until about 2 p.m. they rest. After this they travel through the forest looking for more food until dusk (at about 6 p.m.) when they sleep.

Gorillas rarely travel much more than 1 km (⅔ mile) in a day, because the leaves and shoots which they eat are plentiful in the forests where they live.

Orang-utans

The word 'orang-utan' means 'wild man of the woods'. Orangs live in forests of the islands of Sumatra and Borneo. Unlike the other great apes they live mostly alone. Although they rarely meet, each orang knows its neighbours, for they live in territories which overlap to some extent.

Orangs spend most of their lives in the trees, where they climb slowly and carefully in search of wild figs. They also eat other sorts of fruit and some leaves and insects. They feed in the morning and evening, and rest through the middle of the day.

Chimpanzees

Chimpanzees dislike being alone. Small groups travel together through the African forests looking for the fruit and leaves

which are their main food. They may also eat insects and grubs, and even hunt young antelopes or monkeys.

Chimpanzee language includes at least 24 sounds each with its special meaning. They also use gestures and facial expressions to give information, mainly about how they are feeling, to other members of the group. Chimpanzees use some tools, such as crumpled leaves as 'sponges' for collecting water, and twigs to 'fish' termites from their nests.

The small groups of chimps often split up and change, for they are part of a much larger number, which forms a clan. These animals wander through an area of about 120 sq km (45 sq miles) of forest, usually avoiding neighbouring clans.

Gibbons

Gibbons are small long-armed apes. They are very agile, swinging hand over hand through the treetops, covering as much as 9 m (30 ft) in a single leap.

Gibbons pair for life. They are not aggressive, but warn their neighbours from their small territories by loud calling. Young gibbons are carried and suckled by their mothers for the first year or so, and then their fathers play a larger part in their care. Babies are spaced two or three years apart. The young stay with their parents for about seven years before leaving to find a mate and territory of their own.

▲ Chimpanzees and other apes have long toes so they can grasp things with their feet. Like us their hands have a thumb which can be pressed against a finger to pick up small items.

◄ Chimpanzees safe in a sleeping nest made from springy branches.

◄ Sumatran orang-utan with young. The young will stay with its mother until about the age of seven. The female will have only three or four young in her life.

Monkeys

To many people monkeys are like joke humans. They are primates like human beings, but it is quite wrong to say that we are descended from monkeys. The ancestor which we share with present-day monkeys probably lived more than 30 million years ago. Monkeys are like us in many ways. Their eyes look forwards as ours do; they can hold things in their hands, and they are intelligent and inquisitive.

There are two main groups of monkeys. Those which live in South America all live in the tree-tops. They are wonderful climbers, and many have prehensile (gripping) tails which they use as an extra hand. The others are found in Africa and the warm parts of Asia. None of these has a prehensile tail, and they are much more varied in their life-styles. Some, like baboons, live mainly on the ground. Others, such as the guenons, live in the trees, but they run along big branches and do not swing with their arms. Some, like the colobus monkeys, rarely leave the tree-tops. They are expert climbers and swing hand over hand from quite small branches.

When they are resting, all of the African and Asian monkeys sit upright. They have areas of hardened skin, called callosities or sitting patches, on their buttocks, which act a bit like built-in cushions.

Almost all monkeys live in a territory which they defend from others of their own kind. Within the group each monkey knows its place, and the leader is rarely challenged. There may be noisy arguments, but the fighters are hardly ever seriously damaged.

▲ The spider monkey's prehensile tail can support its total body-weight. It is like an extra hand, very sensitive with naked skin and sweat glands.

◀ Squirrel monkey mother with her young. Squirrel monkeys are found throughout South America. They feed on fruit and insects.

New World monkey   Old World monkey

◄ South American (New World) monkeys have flat noses with nostrils set wide apart and opening to the side. African and Asian (Old World) monkeys' nostrils are closer together.

Distribution
Africa, Asia and Central and South America

Largest
Mandrill, which has a shoulder height of over 50 cm and may weigh over 50 kg

Smallest
Pygmy marmoset, which has a head and body length as little as 12 cm, and weight of about 110 g

Number of young 1

Lifespan
Unknown for most species in the wild. In captivity a baboon has lived for over 35 years.

Female monkeys usually give birth to one baby every few years. The pregnancy lasts about 6 months, and young are nearly always born at night. This protects mothers from predators. The young are carried by their mother, at first clinging to her underside and later riding on her back. They develop slowly, and in most species are not adult for several years. Macaques, for example, reach adulthood at about seven years.

Monkeys and humans

Some monkeys have learned to profit from human activity and have become pests, raiding crops. In India, monkeys are sacred animals and are protected, but in many parts of the world monkeys are now becoming very rare. This is partly because they are hunted for food, for their skins and sometimes for use in laboratories, but mostly because of the destruction of the forests in which they live.

Other primates

The primate order, to which monkeys belong, also includes the lemurs of Madagascar, the pottos and bushbabies of Africa, and the lorises of Asia. These are in a group called the prosimians. The name comes from the Latin for 'early monkeys'. Apes and humans are also primates. Most primates are social creatures living in family groups. They are omnivores, which means they eat a wide range of things, such as fruit, leaves, insects, birds' eggs and some small vertebrates.

◄ Male mandrill, the largest of the monkeys. His bright facial colouring helps to intimidate predators, and other males. The female has similar colouring but it is much duller.

Cats

Cats are among our favourite pets. They were first tamed by the ancient Egyptians at least 3,500 years ago. Now there are many breeds of domestic cat, which people have taken all over the world. They may look very different from each other. Some, such as the Persian cat, have long, fluffy hair and a short face. Others, such as the Siamese cat, have short, smooth fur and a long face and long legs. Domestic cats vary greatly in colour. They may be black, grey, white or various shades of brown, or a mixture of these colours. Their eyes may be golden, green or blue. Yet all kinds of pet cats can breed together. This shows that they all belong to the same kind (species) of animal and have all descended from the same wild ancestor.

Distribution
Domestic cats found on all continents

Size
Up to 25 cm tall at shoulder

Weight
Most weigh between 2·7 kg and 7 kg

Number of young
About 3–5

Lifespan
12–15 years

▶ Your cat behaves like its wild cat relatives. The garden is the jungle where it hunts. Its Latin name is *Felis sylvestris catus*.

The cat family

Pet cats are members of the cat family. This is a group of 37 species including the great cats such as the lion, and the small cats such as the ocelot. Whatever their size, it is easy to see that they are closely related to each other.

Hunting and feeding

All wild cats are hunters depending almost entirely on their kills for food. They all have lithe bodies and strong legs, for their method of hunting is to ambush their prey and then make a brief dash or pounce for the kill. Most cats are very fast over a short distance, but give up if their quarry runs for more than a few metres.

They have large, forward-looking eyes set in the front of the face. This gives them the ability to judge distances accurately as they leap onto prey. A cat's toes carry sharp claws. These are normally sheathed in the pads of the foot so that they are not blunted as the animal runs, but they can be pushed out to hold and tear food.

When it has made a kill a cat wastes no time in eating its meal. At the back of its mouth it has scissor-like teeth which it uses for slicing its food. Like most flesh eaters, cats swallow huge pieces of meat which they can digest easily.

◄ Siberian lynx yawning, showing its 28 teeth (most cats have 30). The small front incisors are for ripping and the large canines for stabbing and tearing. Its back teeth act like scissor blades for slicing meat off the bone.

Many cats hunt at night and have large whiskers which help their sense of touch in the dark.

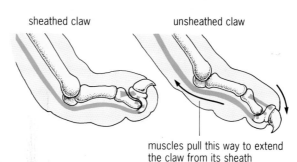

sheathed claw   unsheathed claw

muscles pull this way to extend the claw from its sheath

◄ A cat can retract its claws into sheaths in its paws so they are not worn and blunted when it walks. During an attack, strong muscles pull against the toe bones on which the claws grow, making them extend, like daggers, from their sheaths.

CARE OF PET CATS

Cats are more independent than most other domestic animals. Even so, they must be fed twice a day on high protein food, for cats need more meat in their diet than most other animals. They usually like to drink milk, but they must have water available as well. Food and water dishes should be cleaned daily.

Although pet cats spend a great deal of time grooming themselves, they need to be brushed to get rid of any loose hair. This is particularly important in the long-haired breeds, where the fur can get tangled or matted if it is not properly cared for. If loose hair is not removed the cat may swallow quite a lot of hair when grooming itself. The hair can form a ball in the cat's stomach, causing vomiting and loss of appetite. If the hairball does not come up by itself surgery may be necessary.

During mild weather fleas can be a problem both to the cat and to you. Fleas can be easily controlled by fitting a flea collar (a collar impregnated with insecticide) around the cat's neck, or by regularly spraying the cat with a flea spray obtained from your vet.

Kittens

Kittens need feeding more frequently than adult cats. They will need four meals a day until they are 3 months old, and then three meals a day until 6 months. As kittens must stay inside until they have had all their first injections, they must learn to use a litter tray. They learn this very quickly as cats instinctively bury their wastes. Unless you want to breed from your cat you should take your kitten to the vet to be neutered (have some of its sex organs removed) at about 6 months.

Wild cats

► The cheetah is the fastest land animal, reaching speeds of up to 96 km/h.

Distribution
All of the continents except for Oceania and Antarctica. They do not occur on some islands.

Largest
Siberian tiger, up to 2·8 m head and body length plus 95 cm tail length. Males may weigh as much as 360 kg.

Other great cats
Lion, leopard, jaguar, snow leopard, cheetah. These cats roar, but they have a throat structure which prevents them from purring except when breathing out.

Smallest
Black-footed cat of South Africa. This has a head and body length of not more than 50 cm and a tail length up to 20 cm. It may weigh as little as 1·5 kg.

Other small cats
European wild cat, Pallas's cat, serval, marbled cat, golden cat, margay, fishing cat, jaguarundi, lynx, cougar. These cats do not roar, but can purr when breathing in as well as when breathing out.

Number of young
About 3 or 4, varies between species

Lifespan
About 20 years in captivity, about 12 in the wild

► The jaguar is slightly larger than the leopard, and found only in Central and South America.

Cats are the most carnivorous of all the carnivores. This means that they feed almost entirely on other animals with backbones. All cats are hunters and their good eyesight plays an important part in this: in good light they see about as well as humans do, but in poor light their vision is six times sharper. Hearing and smell are also important but their sense of smell is less well developed than in the dog family. There are seven species of big cat and 28 species of small cat.

Cheetahs

Cheetahs are animals of the grassy plains and are now very rare. They hunt the smaller antelopes and the young of some larger ones. Cheetahs are the fastest moving of all mammals and often run down their prey with a tremendous burst of speed. A cheetah can sprint at about 96 km/h (60 mph) but only for a short time. An average chase lasts 20 seconds. A cheetah's claws are blunt, so it kills its prey by knocking it off balance and throttling it. This is very successful and about half of its chases end in a kill.

Jaguars

The jaguar's beautiful blotched coat camouflages it in the South American forests, where it is usually found near water. It is a good swimmer and sometimes feeds on fish. Jaguars live alone in large territories. A female requires at least 25 sq km (10 sq miles) and a male takes much more. The home ranges overlap, but neighbours avoid each other. They are active mainly at night, when they hunt large ground prey such as peccaries, capybaras or tapirs. They sometimes even catch crocodiles. Jaguars are themselves hunted by humans for their fur and because they may attack cattle.

Leopards

Leopards live in much of Africa and Asia in forests, grasslands and even deserts. They climb trees very well and often rest up in the branches. They also hide the remains of their meals in trees, out of reach of most scavengers. Occasionally a leopard will drop straight down on its prey as it passes beneath the tree. They mainly hunt medium-sized grazing animals such as small antelopes and pigs, but they will resort to smaller prey such as rabbits, rats or even insects.

The patterns on a leopard's coat can vary a lot. One of the most striking variations is where the leopard is totally black. Scientists used to think this was a separate species, and called it the black panther.

Leopards usually live alone. Males defend large territories, but these often overlap the living areas of some females. Cubs may be born at any time of the year and are normally cared for by their mother alone, although sometimes the father helps find food for them. They remain with the adults until they are up to two years old.

Leopards are far rarer than they used to be. Their homes have been destroyed and they have been hunted for their beautiful skins. Now they are protected in some places, so their numbers may increase.

Pumas

The puma is sometimes called the cougar or the mountain lion. Although it may be as big as a leopard or jaguar it is more closely related to the small cats.

Pumas live alone. They do not have fixed dens, but travel through their territories, which are usually over 30 sq km (12 sq miles). They have very powerful hind legs, and it is said that they can leap upwards more than 5 m (16 ft).

Pumas catch beavers, porcupines or hares, but their main prey is deer, usually sick or old animals. They make about one kill a week, and drag the carcass to a safe place to be eaten over several days.

At one time pumas lived in more habitats in North and South America than any other animal. So long as there was cover and prey, they were found in forests and swamps, deserts and mountains and plains. But they have been destroyed in many of these places and now live mainly in remote areas where there are few humans.

▲ The leopard is the most widespread wild member of the cat family, but like all the others it is getting rarer.

◄ The puma is the biggest member of the cat family found in North America. It is active mainly at twilight, feeding on anything from mice to adult deer.

Lions

▶Male lion in his prime. The mane, which darkens with age, gives the impression of great size without much extra weight.

Cubs may be born at any time of the year, though all the females in a pride usually give birth at about the same time. The cubs are fed and looked after by their aunts as well as their mother. They begin hunting by the time they are eleven months old, but are not able to look after themselves fully until they are at least two.

The lionesses do most of the hunting. Sometimes two or more work together to stalk the antelope or zebra which are their main food. Often they fail and only one in four hunts is successful. An adult male may eat 40 kg (90 lb) of meat in a single meal, but then he will probably not feed again for several days.

At one time lions lived in open country through much of Africa, the Middle East and India. Now they have disappeared from most of this vast area, mainly because of destruction of their habitat but also because of relentless hunting. A few hundred remain in one reserve in India; the rest live in Africa where their numbers have fallen by half in 30 years. There are now twice as many lions in captivity as in the wild.

Distribution
Africa, very few in India

Size
Adult male head and body length 2·6–3·3 m, tail length 0·6–1·0 m, height at shoulder about 1·2 m

Weight 150–250 kg

Number of young
3–4 cubs, weaned at 6–7 months and not independent until over 2 years old

Lifespan
In captivity up to 30 years; about 15 years in the wild

Lions live in grassland or scrub country, in groups, called prides. A pride usually consists of about a dozen animals. At least two of them are adult males, the rest females and their cubs. The females in a pride are usually sisters, and remain together all their lives. The males rarely stay with the same pride for more than three years.

▶ Most unusual in mammals, lionesses will suckle other cubs as well as their own. These cubs will lose their spotted fur by about 6 months of age.

Tigers

Tigers are the largest of the big cats. At one time they were found in forest country throughout much of eastern and southern Asia, but now they survive mainly in India and Sumatra. The biggest tigers come from the forests of Siberia. Unlike lions and cheetahs, the tiger is not found living in open habitats.

Male tigers live alone in large territories, though these may overlap the living areas of several females. They warn other males away by roaring when near the boundaries of their living areas. They are chiefly active at twilight or at night, using their sight and sense of hearing rather than smell, to stalk their prey. They may travel up to 20 km (12 miles) in a night and can leap as much as 10 m (30 ft) in a single bound. Tigers are good swimmers and can climb quite well. Their main food is large mammals such as wild pigs, buffalo and deer. But in spite of their size and strength, tigers fail in about 90 per cent of their hunts. Tigers rarely attack humans, but those that do often get a taste for it.

Tiger cubs can be born at any time throughout the year. They do not hunt for themselves until the age of about eighteen months, and they stay with their mother

◀ Siberian tigers are the largest of the species. Like all tigers they like to be near water.

Distribution
India, China, Siberia, Indonesia

Size
Head and body length 140–280 cm; tail length 60–90 cm

Weight
180–360 kg

Number of young
3–4 cubs

Lifespan
In captivity up to 26 years, about 15 in the wild

until they are two or three years old. The male takes no part in rearing his young. He may even kill cubs when taking over another male's territory. If the female's cubs are killed she becomes ready to mate again.

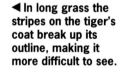

◀ In long grass the stripes on the tiger's coat break up its outline, making it more difficult to see.

Dogs

chihuahua   Afghan hound   cocker spaniel   Airedale   cairn terrier   bulldog   chow chow   bouviers

▲ **The variety amongst breeds of dogs is enormous; yet they all share a common ancestor, the wolf.**

▼ **African wild dogs live and hunt in packs. Packs usually contain about seven adults, and with pups a pack may include as many as 30 dogs.**

Dogs were the first animals to be domesticated and they are now found wherever there are human beings. They vary more in size and appearance than any other animal. They may have short, smooth hair like dobermans; curly fur like poodles; long hair like Afghan hounds, or even no hair like the Mexican hairless dog. But whether they are huge like a Great Dane or tiny like a chihuahua, all dogs belong to the same species. They all have the same basic senses of sight, which is fairly good; hearing, which is very good, and smell which is excellent. They all have the same biological makeup and behaviour patterns and are capable of interbreeding, producing cross-breeds (mongrels).

The differences between breeds are the result of selective breeding by humans. All dogs are descended from the same wild ancestor, the wolf. All are essentially hunters, ready to chase prey. Like all hunters, dogs are intelligent animals, which is why pet dogs that are not given enough to do often become bored and destructive. Like wolves, dogs are pack animals, obedient to the leader of their group. This is one reason why they have taken so well to domestication, where people become the leaders of the pack.

Domestication

The domestication of dogs began towards the end of the Old Stone Age. The humans of that time were very wasteful hunters and wolves must often have been attracted to their rubbish tips. Sometimes a wolf cub might be found and kept. Humans must soon have discovered that a live wolf could be more useful than a dead one, for wolves can run faster than people, and could help them in hunting such animals as bison or wild horses. It took several thousand years to transform wild wolves into tame dogs, but by about 10,000 years ago dogs played an important part in the lives of people.

The first use for dogs was hunting. Wolves hunt largely by sight, and some of the most ancient breeds of hunting dogs, such as

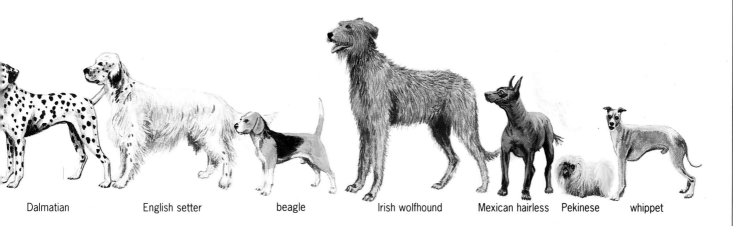

Dalmatian   English setter   beagle   Irish wolfhound   Mexican hairless   Pekinese   whippet

Afghans and greyhounds, are called 'gaze hounds' because they use their eyes, not their noses, for finding prey. All wild dogs have a good sense of smell. Though they use it largely to communicate with each other, it can help in hunting, and we now have many breeds of dog, such as blood-hounds and foxhounds, which hunt by scent.

A very useful companion

Once dogs had been tamed it was possible to use their hunting instinct to herd animals, and not kill them. Herding was another early use for dogs, and one which is still important today. Wolves defend their territories, so dogs could easily be trained to guard the human living places that they shared. Wolves also defend their pack. In ancient times large breeds of dogs were used for fighting in battles, defending their human pack. Large dogs, such as bouviers, were often used to pull small carts, and in the Arctic, sledge dogs were vital to human survival.

Sometimes very small dogs were born. They were kept for an important function: that of being a mobile hot water bottle! A dog's normal temperature is higher than that of a human being, and in days before central heating, people often kept themselves warm by cuddling small dogs, called 'lap dogs'.

Nowadays we understand a great deal about dog behaviour, and it is possible to train dogs to a much higher standard than ever before. So dogs have new work with

humans. Some are guide dogs for the blind and hearing dogs for the deaf. Others are trained as sniffer dogs to help defeat terrorists and drug dealers, and disaster dogs, trained to find people buried in avalanches or the rubble of earthquakes.

CARE OF PET DOGS

Think very carefully before getting a dog. Dogs can live for about 15 years, and in that time they will need feeding, grooming and exercise every single day.

Most adult dogs are happy with one main meal a day, and any of the good quality shop-bought dog foods will provide a nutritionally balanced diet. Puppies need more frequent feeding: four times a day before 3 months, then three times a day till 6 months.

All dogs need exercise. The amount of exercise needed depends on the breed of the dog and its age. Very old dogs and puppies require less exercise than a dog in its prime. A puppy's walks should be gradually lengthened to allow it to build up muscle. Exercise for any dog should be regular: a short walk around the block during the week and a four-hour walk on Sunday is not a good programme.

Tallest
Irish wolfhound, shoulder height about 110 cm

Heaviest
St Bernard, weight about 100 kg

Smallest
Chihuahua weighs under 1 kg

Fastest
Over long distance, saluki; over short distances, greyhound

Number of young
3–10

Lifespan
Usually longer than 10 years, although very large breeds and very small ones tend not to live so long. Longest-lived dog on record over 27 years. Species of wild dog include African hunting dog, bush dog, dhole, racoon dog, and maned wolf.

◄ **Sheepdog herding sheep. One of the many examples of how dogs are still as useful today as they have been at any time in the past.**

Wild dogs

Distribution
Virtually worldwide (in some areas, such as Madagascar and New Zealand there is only the domestic dog)

Largest
Grey wolf: up to 2 m in length and 80 kg in weight

Smallest
Fennec fox: about 24 cm in length and 0·8 kg in weight

Number of young
About 4, but varies between species

Lifespan
Up to between 6 and 10 years in the wild, more in captivity

Most members of the dog family have lithe bodies, long legs and bushy tails. They are mainly social animals living in groups.

Foxes

Unlike most members of the dog family, foxes live alone, although cubs born in the spring remain with both parents through the summer. The red fox is found over more of the world than any other carnivore (flesh-eater). It can survive from the Arctic tundra through grassland to temperate forests, and has recently discovered that it can make a good living in towns and suburbs, close to human beings.

The red fox can survive on a wide variety of foods, such as small rodents, rabbits, insects, earthworms and carrion. It also eats fruit, and in season wild berries, apples and rosehips can make up 90 per cent of its diet. Some foxes do a lot of damage killing game birds and raiding hen runs, but most do not, and their usefulness in killing pests generally outweighs any harm. In spite of this, they are hunted and trapped in many areas. They have very good sight, hearing

and sense of smell, and can also run fast (up to 48 km/h or 30 mph) over long distances, jumping obstacles and swimming through water.

Most other species of fox live in more specialized environments, but are otherwise similar to the red fox.

Jackals

Jackals live in warm, dry, open country. The golden jackal may be found close to towns or villages, where it scavenges. But in general jackals feed on rodents, lizards, ground-living birds and insects, although they are capable of hunting larger animals, up to the size of small antelopes. They also take fruit and carrion, including leftovers from lions' kills.

Jackals normally live in pairs, although they may come together in groups where food is abundant. Once mated they usually remain together, occupying a hunting area of several square kilometres, which includes a defended territory, marked with urine. The cubs are born in an underground

▶ **Red fox cubs are reared by both parents, who feed them and guard them while they play. They sometimes bring injured animals so the cubs can learn to make a kill.**

◄ Black-backed jackals eating a seal pup on the Namib coast. The jackal on the left of the group is letting the others know he is not a threat, by his submissive posture.

▼ Most wolves live in packs. This lone grey wolf is probably a young animal looking for territory or a mate.

den within the territory. They stay with their parents for six month or longer, helping to rear the next year's litter.

Jackals are accused of killing farm stock and so are hunted. Because of this and the destruction of their habitat, simien jackals are now an endangered species.

Wolves

Wolves live in packs the size of which depends on food availability. The pack centres around the breeding pair (which mate for life) and can contain up to twenty members. Because they hunt as a group, wolves are able to kill animals larger than themselves, and feed mostly on deer, moose and caribou, usually preying on the weaker ones. After making a kill, a wolf can eat about 9 kg (20 lb) of meat. The pack will finish the carcass completely.

To find enough food wolf packs need very large home ranges. If prey is quite scarce the wolves must roam an area as large as 1,000 sq km (400 sq miles). The wolf is becoming increasingly rarer as its habitat is destroyed and it is hunted by humans.

Most stories of wolves attacking humans are greatly exaggerated. Many came about after wars or famine, when wolves were seen scavenging on corpses.

Weasels

Otters

Otters are more at home in the water than on land. Kept warm and waterproof by their dense coats, otters can close their nostrils and remain under water for six minutes. The otter's stream-lined shape enables it to swim at speeds of up to 12 km (7½ miles) per hour. The huge whiskers feel movements in the water so that it can hunt in murky streams or in the dark.

River otters hunt small fish, frogs and other water animals, which they catch in their mouths. Clawless otters, which live in tropical Asia and in Africa, use their sensitive fingers to feel in mud or under stones for shrimps and crabs.

Sea otters, which live off the west coast of North America, also use their forefeet to capture their prey. This includes slow-swimming fishes, sea urchins and molluscs. To break open the shells the sea otter rests a stone on its chest. It then bangs the shell on this anvil until it is cracked. Sea otters are the only mammals except primates to use a tool of any sort.

Badgers

Badgers are shy, nocturnal creatures. They are good diggers, using the long claws on their forelimbs to dig out food or make burrows called sets. European badgers usually live in groups of up to twelve animals in sets which may be occupied for many generations. An ancient set can contain over 100 m (300 ft) of tunnels, and a large number of entrance holes and sleeping chambers.

Badgers are generally peaceable creatures. In spite of their powerful teeth they feed mostly on small prey and plants. Their eyesight is poor, but they have excellent senses of hearing and smell. Badgers have special musk glands under their tails and with these they scent-mark familiar objects.

▲ One of the smallest carnivores, the European weasel kills prey larger than itself.

Distribution
All continents except Australia and Antarctica

Largest
Giant otter: up to 90 cm; weight up to 30 kg.

Smallest
Weasel (least weasel), females as little as 15 cm and weigh as little as 25 g

Number of young 1–5

Lifespan
A Canadian otter survived 26 years in captivity; weasels live about 1 year

Members of the weasel family are generally long-bodied, short-legged hunters. They live in many ways: the martens, for instance, are tree climbers, the otters are swimmers and the badgers are diggers. In Europe the animal known as 'the weasel' is the smallest of the family. Females are said to be able to squeeze through a wedding ring! They are often active during the daytime, for though they hunt mainly by scent, they have good senses of hearing and sight.

Weasels feed mainly on small rodents, and in the northern part of their range they are tiny enough to be able to chase mice and voles down their tunnels. The prey is killed with a bite to the base of the skull. When food is plentiful it is sometimes stored.

Pandas

◀ One of the rarest of mammals, the giant panda. There may be as few as 500 left in the wild.

Distribution
Giant panda, mountains of central China; red panda, parts of the northern Himalayas and mountains of south central China

Size
Giant panda 120–150 cm, weight 75–160 kg; red panda, head and body length up to 60 cm, tail length up to 48 cm, weight up to 4·5 kg

Number of young
Up to 2 or 3 (giant panda never rears more than one)

Lifespan
Giant panda over 26 years in captivity; red panda over 13 years in captivity

Two different sorts of animals are both called pandas. The giant panda is usually classified with the bears, and the red or lesser panda with the racoons, although some biologists think the pandas should be in a separate family of their own.

Giant pandas

The giant panda is one of the rarest and most striking animals in the world. Few people have seen pandas alive except in zoos. Pandas rarely breed in captivity.

Giant pandas live only in high mountains in three isolated parts of China. Groups of pandas may be seen in the breeding season, but at other times they live alone.

Giant pandas take up to twelve hours a day chewing the tough shoots and roots of bamboo, which are their main diet. They have an extra bone in their hands which they use much as we use our thumbs, so they are able to grasp their food. Although they do eat other plants, and occasionally hunt small mammals and birds, many pandas starve if the bamboo crop fails.

The rarity of giant pandas has little to do with human activity. It is mainly because of changes in climate and vegetation since the end of the last ice age. Because of strict conservation they may survive for longer than many other rare mammals.

Red pandas

Red pandas live in mountain forests in China and parts of the Himalayas. Family parties often stay together, sleeping by day in tree dens. At night, when they feed, they stay mainly on the ground, searching for fruits, acorns and plant shoots and sometimes catching insects and small vertebrates.

◀ The red or lesser panda is about the size of a large domestic cat. It is an excellent climber, and is more widespread than the giant panda.

Bears

Bears are the largest flesh-eating land mammals: the biggest bear weighs more than three times as much as a large lion. Bears will sometimes kill large animals but they are mostly omnivorous, feeding on both plants and small creatures.

Bears can swim well and young ones can climb trees, but as they grow older, they do so less. Bears have poor eyesight and hearing, but their sense of smell is excellent. They generally live alone, though groups may sometimes come together in places where there is plenty of food.

In the autumn, when food is abundant, bears grow very fat. Then they find a secure den in which they snooze away the winter months. They do not go into a deep hibernation, and it is at this time that females produce their young. The cubs are very small, less than 1 per cent of their mother's weight. They emerge from the den after several months, when food is becoming plentiful.

Polar bears

Polar bears live in the icy wastes of the Arctic. They feed mainly on seals, which they catch by laying in wait at their breathing holes, or at the water's edge, and spearing them with their sharp claws, when they come up to breathe. Polar bear cubs are born in December and January in dens dug in drifted snow. At birth they weigh only about 600g (21 oz); their mother can weigh up to 300 kg (660 lb). Polar bear milk is very high in fat so the cubs grow quickly in the four months spent in the safety of the den. They remain with their mothers for 28 months.

◄ **Polar bears are not often found together, but sometimes ice-free conditions force them ashore and they may form groups.**

Distribution
Europe, Asia, South
America, North America
and the Arctic. Only the
spectacled bear of the
Andes is found south of
the Equator.

Largest
Polar bear: head and body
length up to 3 m; weight
up to 800 kg

Smallest
Sun bear: head and body
length up to 1·4 m; weight
27–65 kg

Number of young 1–4

Lifespan
15–30 years in the wild,
much longer in captivity

◀ **Grizzly bear fishing
for salmon. Grizzlies
fish using their teeth or
claws. They take the
fish ashore to eat them.**

Grizzly bears

Grizzly bears are the most widely distributed
species of all the bears, although their
numbers are rapidly dwindling. Their diet
consists largely of vegetation, including
tubers which they dig up with their sharp
claws, and berries. They also feed on insect
grubs, rodents, fish, carrion and young
deer. Grizzlies eat up to 16 kg (35 lb) of
food a day when not in hibernation.

The young are born between January and
March in the female's den (maybe a natural
cave or a hollow tree). They are quite hairless and helpless at birth. They may remain
with their mother for as long as four years.

Small bears

There are four species of small bear, all of
which tend to be black in colour. As with
the larger bears they feed mostly on plant
material, though the sloth bear also spends
a lot of time eating termites. Sun bears, the
smallest bears, and spectacled bears do not

hibernate and may breed at any time of the
year. Sun bears are thought to mate for life,
and so are sloth bears. As with the larger
bear species, all small bears are endangered.

▶ **The Himalayan black
bear, one of the smallest
bears, is a good climber.
It often climbs trees in
search of nuts and fruit.**

Domestic animals

▼ Longhorn cattle are a very old cattle breed. They were used in the first livestock breeding programme, in the 18th century.

Most of the animals we are close to are domestic animals: they are tame and breed easily in captivity. All domestic animals were originally bred from wild species.

Cattle feed mostly during the daytime, each eating about 70 kg (150 lb) of grass, but they also browse on trees and shrubs. They are cud-chewing animals, which means they have complicated stomachs, made up of four parts. Grasses and other leaves are eaten, without much chewing, and swallowed into the rumen and reticulum where they are partly broken down (digested) by millions of bacteria. The animal then 'chews the cud' by passing food back into its mouth and chewing it thoroughly. Chewed food is swallowed into the reticulum, then passes into the omasum and abomasum where more microbes complete digestion.

Cattle were first domesticated about 8,000 years ago. Today there are about 200 breeds, which vary in size and colour. Some, such as the Jerseys, have been bred for the rich milk that they produce, and others for their meat and hides. Cattle are also used for pulling ploughs and heavy loads, and in some parts of the world their dried droppings are important as fuel.

Cattle

Cattle were originally wild, woodland animals. Few are left in the wild now, as their forests have been destroyed, but the banteng and the gaur still survive in the forests of south-east Asia. In the wild the bull leads a group of about fifteen cows and their calves. The ancestor of almost all domestic cattle, the aurochs, became extinct in 1627. Wild species of cattle called the banteng and the gaur still survive in very small numbers in the forests of south-east Asia. In the wild the bull leads a group of about fifteen cows and their calves.

Pigs

Wild pigs have a coat of harsh hair, which is generally red-brown or grey in colour, unlike domestic pigs, most of which are smooth-skinned or possess only a few coarse bristles. Except for the warthog, which comes from the savannahs of Africa, most pigs are forest animals. They are usually seen in small groups or family parties, although peccaries, which live in Central America, sometimes occur in large herds. Most pigs make a short burrow, roughly lined with twigs or grass, in which they rest or hide.

Sows (females) produce their litter of five or six young in their burrow. The piglets are helpless at birth, and they remain in the lair for the first few days of their life. When young they are camouflaged with stripes and spots, but these are lost as they grow.

Distribution
Virtually worldwide

Largest
Cattle, about 1·8 m at the shoulder; up to 900 kg in weight

Smallest
Pygmy hog, about 58 cm long and weighing as little as 6 kg

Number of young
1 for most species, but pigs have between 4 and 8 young

Lifespan
Over 20 years (less for pigs)

▶ Cows have complicated stomachs. Their food is returned to the mouth to be chewed again after it has been swallowed.

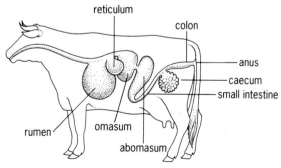

reticulum

colon

anus

caecum

small intestine

rumen

omasum

abomasum

◄ Wild boar with
piglets. Pigs are
intelligent and very
adaptable.

Unlike most of their cloven-hoofed relatives, such as cattle, pigs do not chew the cud. They feed on grasses and ground-living plants, and often use their long snouts, which are strengthened with a special bone, to dig up roots. The European wild boar is the ancestor of the domestic pig.

Sheep

Wild sheep live in mountainous areas. They are good climbers, but are less agile than their cousins the goats, so they are generally found at lower and less rocky levels. Both males and females have horns, which are usually curled into a flat spiral. The horns of the males are larger and are used particularly in fighting for mates. Like goats, wild sheep are wary, tough animals, with dense hairy coats. In the winter-time they grow a thick undercoat (fleece) of fine wool and this helps to keep them warm and dry in even the harshest weather. It is moulted completely in the summer.

A wild ewe about to have her lamb leaves the small group with which she normally lives and finds a safe ledge. The lamb remains there with her for several days after birth. At this time its main enemies

are eagles, but later it may have many enemies including humans. Largely because of over-hunting most kinds of wild sheep are now very rare.

The value of the winter woolly coat for making warm clothing and carpets meant that people kept and bred from sheep which retained their wool into the summer-time. Today, most domestic breeds have lost their hairy coats and have only the woolly fleece. This is not shed, but has to be sheared.

The mouflon, a wild sheep from south-west Asia, was domesticated about 9,000 years ago. Today it is an endangered species. There are now more than 800 breeds and over 680 million domestic sheep. They have been taken by humans to many parts of the world and millions of sheep are reared every year in New Zealand, Australia and North and South America.

Goats

Wild goats and their relatives, such as the chamois, are cloven-hoofed animals that feed on plants, chewing the cud as cows do. They live in herds in many mountainous parts of Europe, Asia and North America. Goats are usually stockily built, with coats made of thick, often coarse hair, to protect them from the cold of their upland homes.

Goats' hooves have a hard rim and a softer inner sole. These act like suction cups as the goats scamper and leap over rocks and ice high up in the mountains.

All wild goats have horns, which may be up to 2 metres long (over 6 ft). They are used in defence, and by the males when fighting for mates. In late spring the females find well-protected ledges, where they produce one or sometimes two well-developed kids. Eagles will kill some of these, but when the kids are strong enough to join the herd they are safe from almost all enemies except for human beings.

The goats of western Asia were among the first animals to be domesticated, about 9,000 years ago. Now there are many varieties of tame goats, kept for milk, meat and skins.

▲ The ibex is a wild goat with a beard and long curved horns. Males have a strong smell, and fight by butting each other with their horns to win females.

Horses

Wild horses in herds live in open country. They can detect predators from a distance with their sharp senses of sight, hearing and smell, and their speed enables them to escape from danger. Today wild horses are very rare, and domesticated horses are used more for pleasure than for work.

Domestication

Horses were first domesticated by pre-historic people in Central Asia over 6,000 years ago. At first, they were used to pull lightweight chariots, but later, when larger breeds had been developed, people began to ride. To begin with they rode without saddles or stirrups. The Roman cavalry were the first to use saddles regularly, but stirrups were unknown through most of Europe until the 9th century AD. Their use spread slowly, and for several hundreds of years after this people continued to ride without them.

Distribution
Middle East to Mongolia, and East Africa. Domestic horses are found through-out the world. Feral horses (domestic horses gone wild) live in many places, especially in America and Australia.

Largest
One Percheron stood 21 hands, and measured more than 500 cm long (any horse over 18 hands is considered very large).

Smallest
The Falabella, adults are between 3 and 10 hands.

Lifespan
Up to 40 years

Horses are measured at the shoulder in hands. One hand measures 4 inches (10·16 cm), the width of a man's knuckles.

▲ Przewalski's horse with foal. This is the wild species ancestral to domestic horses, and they survived in eastern Asia until the 1950s. They are probably now extinct in the wild, though several herds are kept in zoos.

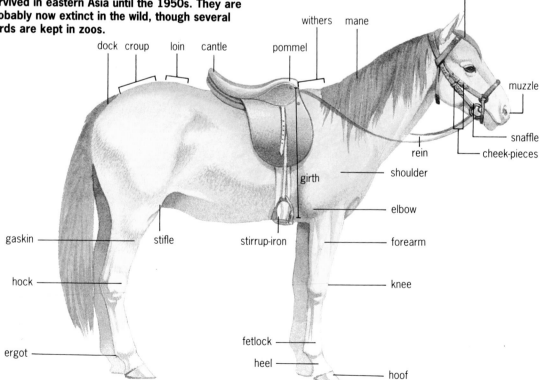

Pack horses were used to carry loads over rough and often roadless country, but donkeys, mules and oxen had to be used for ploughing and dragging heavy loads. It was not until the invention of the horse collar, which came from Asia to Europe in about AD 900, that horses could be used to pull heavy weights.

During the Middle Ages, the armour worn by knights was so heavy that only very big horses could stand their weight. Huge animals, called the great horses, were bred. These became the ancestors of today's heavy horses, such as the Shires. Lighter-weight, speedier horses were bred in the countries surrounding the Mediterranean Sea. These were the ancestors of the fast, slender-limbed horses, such as the Arab breeds and thoroughbreds of today.

Ponies

A pony is a small horse, standing less than 14 hands (142 cm or about 4 ft 8 in) at the withers (the ridge between its shoulder blades). The wild ancestors of all domestic horses, Przewalski's horses, are only about this size, but once they were tamed, larger and stronger horses were bred. In some areas, particularly in the northern parts of the world, some of these horses escaped or were allowed to roam into wild country. Those that survived were small, thrifty animals that could manage on little feed. In time, within each remote area slightly different types of ponies developed. But they all tended to be sturdy and independent, and these are characteristics that are found in ponies today.

Colt
A male horse less than four years old.
Filly
A female horse less than four years old.
Yearling
A horse between one and two years old.
Gelding
A male horse that has been castrated and so cannot be used for breeding.
Stallion
A male horse that can be used for breeding.
Mare
A female horse over four years old.

EVOLUTION

The earliest known ancestor of the horse was a creature called *Hyracotherium*. It lived about 58 million years ago in tropical forests in Europe and America. It was about the size of a miniature poodle dog, and different in shape and habits from modern horses.

Many kinds of fossil horses have been discovered, and these show us how horses have evolved. Changes took place in size, and in foot shape so that horses became better runners. Other changes took place in the shape of their teeth, so that they were able to eat tough grasses rather than soft leaves.

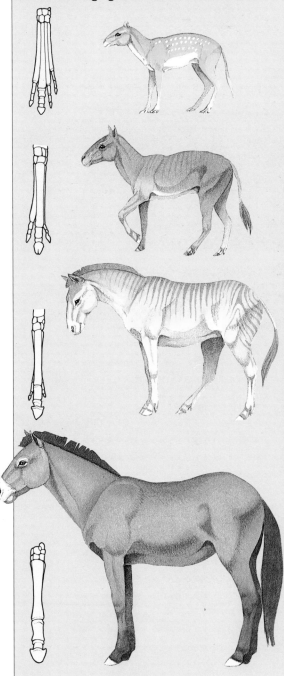

◄ *Hyracotherium*, sometimes called *Eohippus* 'dawn horse', lived about 58 million years ago in warm forests. It ran on its toes, like a dog, and had four toes on the front feet and three on the hind, each with a broad, hoof-like claw.

◄ *Mesohippus* was a forest dweller of about 36 million years ago. Larger than *Hyracotherium*, it lengthened its stride by running on the tips of its toes. It had three toes on each foot, which were protected by large toenails.

◄ *Merychippus* was the first plains horse and lived about 25 million years ago. It had three toes on each foot, but only the middle toe normally touched the ground. Its teeth were suited for eating grass and its eyes were positioned to see danger from afar.

◄ *Equus* is the Latin name of modern wild and domestic horses. They are fast-running, grass-feeding animals that live on dry plains. They have only one toe on each foot; this is protected by a large wrap-around toenail called a hoof.

Zebras

▶ Large numbers of plains zebras still survive in some parts of Africa. A herd consists of many family groups and the adults in each group stay together for the rest of their lives.

Distribution
Savannah and dry scrub areas from Ethiopia to South Africa

Size
Head and body length 200–240 cm; shoulder height 120–140 cm

Weight
About 350 kg; Grevy's zebra is the largest species.

Number of young
1 suckled for about 7 months

Lifespan Up to 25 years

Zebras have been called 'ponies in pyjamas', for these African wild horses are covered with black and white stripes. No two zebras have the same arrangement of stripes. A herd of plains zebras consists of many families and they recognize members of their own family and their neighbours by their different patterns.

As a family moves it keeps a strict order. A mare (adult female) leads. She is the dominant female and is followed by her foals. Behind her comes the next most dominant mare, and so on. In a big family, there may be as many as six mares. Right at the back comes the stallion, who is the father of all of the foals. If there is a weak or injured member of the family it will be protected by the whole group, who go slowly so that it is not left behind. The stallion fights off predators, such as lions, and sometimes loses his life so that his family can escape.

When a foal is being born the stallion stands near by to protect the mare. The foal is able to move around within an hour of birth. A female zebra will leave the group at around the age of two when a bachelor male steals her. She will join and leave several groups before she finally settles down in the group where she will spend the rest of her life. She will have her first foal at around four years old and after that may have a foal each year.

Young males leave their family and join a bachelor group when they are about four years old. They will take over a family of their own by the age of about six.

When they are not grazing, zebras spend a lot of time nibbling each other's fur. This not only keeps them clean, but is part of their social life.

The mountain zebra and Grevy's zebra are much rarer than the plains zebra, and live in drier, more remote country. Mountain zebras also live in family groups but Grevy's zebras have a far less complex social life.

Giraffes

can run at speeds of about 55 km/h (34 mph). If they are cornered they protect themselves by kicking with their powerful feet. Males sometimes fight, swinging their heads to thump each other's sides. This makes a loud thud, though they seem to do little harm. The bone of a giraffe's head continues to thicken throughout its life. The giraffe is born with small horns which grow larger as it gets older. This is more obvious in males: an adult male's skull may weigh three times as much as that of an adult female.

Giraffe calves

The female goes to a traditional calving ground to give birth to her calf. This is where all her calves will have been born, and those of many other females too. A male calf is about 1·9 m (6·34 ft) tall at birth, and weighs about 102 kg (209 lb). Female calves are slightly smaller. By age 2 young males have doubled in height.

Okapis

Giraffes have a short-necked cousin, the okapi, which lives in the dense forest of Zaïre. Okapis were found in 1901, the last large mammals to be discovered. Still very little is known of their behaviour.

Distribution
Africa south of the Sahara

Size
Up to 5·3 m in height; about 800 kg in weight

Number of young 1

Lifespan
26 years is the longest known in the wild; over 36 years in captivity

◀ **Coat patterns in giraffes vary enormously, from the large, regular patches separated by white lines, of these reticulated giraffes, to the smaller jagged 'spots' of the Masai giraffe.**

▼ **A female okapi. Males have skin-covered horns like the giraffe.**

Giraffes are the tallest of all mammals. They live in the African savannah, where their good eyesight and their height enable them to see for great distances. A small herd of giraffes may be scattered over several square kilometres without losing contact with each other.

Giraffes' long necks enable them to reach food too high for other ground-living animals. Their necks may be as much as 2 m in length, but are still made up of only seven bones as in most other mammals. Giraffes usually feed early or late in the day, and rest and chew the cud in the heat of the afternoon. They must spend about twelve hours a day feeding. Giraffes are timid animals and run from danger. They

Antelopes

▶Female and male (with horns) impala. Males and females usually only come together to breed.

Distribution
African grasslands mainly, but also forests, deserts and swamps and the cold steppes of Asia

Largest antelope
Eland, shoulder height up to 1·8 m; weight up to 1,000 kg

Smallest antelopes
Royal and Bates's pygmy antelopes, which are about 30 cm at the shoulder and weigh about 3 kg

Number of young
1 per year in the larger species; smaller antelopes breed more often.

Lifespan
Over 23 years for eland, over 10 years for one of the small species

Antelopes may be as big as cows or as small and delicate as new-born lambs. They are all long-legged, cloven-hoofed animals that feed on plants. Like cows they chew the cud.

▶Wildebeest (also called gnus) can still be found in vast herds from southern Africa to Kenya.

Most antelopes live in large herds. Often a herd consists of only females and calves, as males form other groups. Males ready to mate generally live alone and will fight other males for territory. Their horns are usually spiral or notched so that the rivals' horns lock together when fighting. This results in a trial of strength as they push each other backwards and forwards. Although the fights look fierce, the loser can easily break free and injuries are rare.

A baby antelope can stand within minutes of being born, and is soon an active member of the herd. It becomes independent quickly, for its mother will produce a new calf in the next year.

Antelopes are the prey of many flesh eaters, but humans are their most dangerous enemy. Many species have now become very rare through over-hunting, or destruction of their habitat. Attempts have been made to domesticate some kinds of antelope, and they may become important farm animals in the future.

Rhinos and hippos

Rhinoceroses

Rhinoceroses are different from all other horned mammals in that their horns are not on the top of the head, but are towards the end of the nose. These horns are not like the horns of cattle, or the antlers of deer, but are made of compressed thick hairs.

Rhinos live in tropical grasslands and forests, always in reach of water, for they need to drink every day and also enjoy wallowing in mud. They feed entirely on plants, which black rhinos pick using a grasping upper lip. They have good senses of hearing and smell, but they are short-sighted. Apart from mothers with calves they usually live alone, and are suspicious of strangers. As a result they may attack intruders without real cause.

In spite of their heavy skin, rhinoceroses are plagued by ticks and other parasites. They are often seen with tick birds, which help the rhinos by feeding on the pests. Baby rhinos may be hunted by the big cats, but man is the only enemy of an adult. In the past dozens of types of rhinoceroses lived in many parts of the world. Today, only five species survive, and all of these have been hunted and poached to near extinction.

◄ White rhinoceroses grazing. Because of their large size rhinos must spend most of the day feeding.

Rhinos

Distribution
Africa and tropical Asia

Size
Up to 5 m in head and body length and weight up to 3,600 kg

Number of young 1

Lifespan
Up to 50 years

Hippopotamuses

'Hippopotamus' means 'river horse'. Hippos do spend much of their time resting in water, but they are more closely related to cattle than horses.

A hippo has good sight, hearing and sense of smell. Its eyes and nostrils are high up on its head, so it can stay hidden just under the water and continue to see and breathe. It closes its nostrils and ears when completely under water. Hippos have glands in their skin which produce droplets of red liquid. This protects the skin from becoming too dry.

Hippos live in groups of females and their young. The babies are well cared for. They sometimes ride on their mothers' backs, perhaps to protect them from crocodiles in the water. The males must compete for territory and females. Hippos leave the water every night to feed. They eat mainly grass, but sometimes raid crops, causing immense damage.

Hippos

Distribution
Rivers and lakes in East Africa and West Africa

Size
Head and body length up to 4·6 m; up to 4,500 kg in weight

Number of young 1

Lifespan
Up to 54 years

◄ Hippos must remain close to water. The surface layer of their skin is thinner than that of other mammals, and so in dry air they lose much more water.

Elephants

For centuries Asian elephants have been used as beasts of burden, carrying or dragging timber and other heavy materials. Elephants are also trained to perform in circuses. African elephants are far more difficult to tame because they are fiercer.

The Asian elephant (below) differs in many ways from its African cousins (right). Asian elephants have small, triangular ears; African elephants have large, rounded ears. Asian elephants have rounded backs; African elephants have concave (hollowed) backs. Asian elephants have two bulges on their foreheads; African elephants have rounded foreheads.

Elephants are the biggest living land animals. There are two types of elephant, African and Asian. Both types live in herds, and have poor eyesight, but very good senses of hearing and smell. If one animal detects danger, the whole herd is alerted.

Elephants do not defend the home range over which they wander; instead they seem to know and be on friendly terms with their neighbours. Each herd is led by an old female who is followed by her young offspring and her adult daughters and their families. The elephants in a herd remain together for many years. Its members keep close to each other and look after and even suckle each other's babies if need be. Sometimes a herd splits, and a younger female leaves with some of the others, but they remain close to the parent group and may rejoin it briefly.

Young males leave the herd when they reach puberty, at the age of about twelve years. Males may form herds, but these do not have any constant members and change from one day to the next. There is no special breeding season, but if a female is ready to mate, her group will be joined by males though they will not remain permanently.

◀ **Asian elephant.**

Trunks and tusks

As well as their size, the two things which set elephants apart from other mammals are their trunks and their tusks. The trunk is the elephant's nose. It is boneless but muscular and has one or two finger-like points at the tip. The elephant uses it to breathe, and to drink, which it does by sniffing water up and then blowing it down its throat. It is also used as a hand, strong enough to break down a branch, and delicate enough to pick a single fruit the size of a raspberry.

An elephant's trunk is very sensitive; courting elephants twine trunks, and mother elephants spend a lot of time using their trunks to touch and fondle their babies. This 'elephant cuddling' is important to the calf. One which is deprived of it does not make such good progress as one which has plenty of contact.

An elephant's tusks are its second upper incisor teeth. When they begin to grow they have a cap of enamel, like human teeth. But as they get larger the enamel does not continue to cover them. The greater part of a tusk is made of dentine (ivory). Elephants use their tusks for defence, and in feeding. They continue to grow throughout the elephant's whole life, so one with very large tusks is likely to be an old animal. Females have smaller tusks than males, and Asian elephant tusks are smaller than those of African elephants.

Feeding

An elephant's size means that, when it is fully grown, it is safe from all predators other than humans. To support its large size it needs huge amounts of food. An adult elephant eats about 150 kg (300 lb) of grass, leaves, twigs and fruit each day.

Such tough food needs to be thoroughly chewed, and elephants have grinding teeth

◄ African elephants.

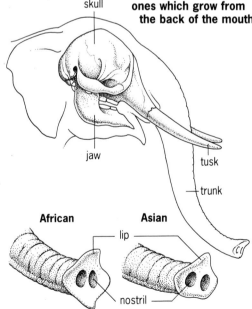

▼ An elephant's skull is up to a quarter of its total body weight. Its front teeth (incisors) form the tusks and its back teeth (molars) fall out when worn down and are replaced by new ones which grow from the back of the mouth.

▲ An elephant's upper lip and nose form its trunk. It is a sense organ of smell and touch; it can squirt water and dust, is strong enough to lift trees, but has one or two finger-like lips which can pick up a tiny pebble.

in the back of their mouths. This is the position in which the teeth have the most force, but they do wear out. When this happens they are replaced by others which push in from behind. In all they have six sets of grinding teeth, but when the last of these wears out, the animal is probably about 55 years old. It becomes weakened by lack of food and dies of starvation or disease.

Endangered species

In the past there were many species of elephants, which lived over most of the world apart from Australia. Some were much bigger than the elephants of today, but they are now all extinct. Today's elephants are also endangered. As a result of hunting for ivory and poaching and taking over the elephants' environment, there are far fewer elephants today than there were even 20 years ago. Many people feel that it is not possible for such large and demanding animals to survive in a world of expanding human populations.

Distribution
Africa south of the Sahara, and south-east Asia

Asian elephant
Head and body length
5·5–6·4 m;
shoulder height 2·5–3·0 m;
weight up to 5,000 kg

African elephant
Head and body length
6·0–7·5 m;
shoulder height 3–4 m;
weight 2,200–7,500 kg

Heaviest single tusk
Weight 107 kg

Number of young
1, very rarely twins. Calf begins to be weaned at about 1 year, but takes some milk until it is about 4 years old.

Lifespan
50–70 years
Elephants are pregnant for 22 months.

Whales and dolphins

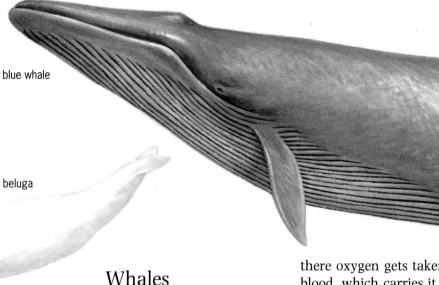

blue whale

beluga

Whales

Whales are mammals. They are warm-blooded, air-breathing creatures, which produce living young and feed them on milk. They are also very intelligent. Whales live all their lives in water, and die if they are forced onto dry land, for their weight crushes their lungs. The term 'whale' is generally used for creatures more than 10 m (30 ft) long, but dolphins and porpoises are also whales.

Breathing

All whales are streamlined. They swim using a horizontal tail fin called a fluke and a pair of large flippers near the front of the body. Inside these flippers are bones similar to those of your arms and hands. Whales have no hind limbs at all. Their skin is very smooth. Unlike most mammals, which have hair or fur, whales have at most a few short, bristly hairs round their jaws. They are kept warm by a layer of blubber beneath the skin. In a big whale, this can be 60 cm (2 ft) thick.

Toothed whales have one nostril; baleen whales have two. The nostrils are on top of the head and called a blowhole. This is the first part of the whale to surface. Air breathed in goes down to the lungs; from

there oxygen gets taken into the blood, which carries it to the muscles. A whale can carry enough oxygen in this way to last over an hour under water. When it comes to the surface, it needs to breathe deeply. As it does so it throws out of its blowhole a foam from its lungs. This foam contains trapped nitrogen from the air. This is mainly what can be seen when a whale 'blows'. The whale does not breathe water out of its blowhole, as a whale with water in its lungs would drown, just like any other mammal. Because it can remove the nitrogen from the air it breathes, a whale can dive deeply and come to the surface quickly. This would kill human divers.

Sight and sound

Whales' eyes are not large, and since they close their nostrils when they submerge, a sense of smell would be of little use to them. Their smooth bodies have no visible ears, but they do actually hear very well indeed. They use sounds we call whale songs, to communicate with each other. Some whale songs carry many hundreds of kilometres under water. They use sound to locate obstacles and food (echolocation). Loud bursts of sound are also used to disable prey. Most whales feed on fishes or squid, but the largest species feed on krill.

Distribution
All of the oceans of the world

Largest
Blue whale: 25–33 m, females slightly larger than males; weight 100–120 tonnes, record weight about 180 tonnes

Smallest
Gulf of California porpoise: 1·2–1·5 m long; weight as little as 30 kg

Number of young 1

Lifespan
Fin and blue whale thought to live for over 110 years; as little as 10 years for the smaller dolphins and porpoises

narwhal

minke whale

Dolphins

Dolphins are small whales, which in most cases have a long snout, crammed with up to 200 small pointed teeth, ideal for catching fishes. Most are creatures of the open sea, though some come into inshore waters.

Four species of dolphins are known as river dolphins, as they live in fresh water in South America, China and India. The Amazon and La Plata dolphins have more of a neck than other whales and are thought to be 'living fossils', because of their similarities with ancient fossil whales.

The true dolphins are slender, streamlined creatures, some of which are capable of swimming at speeds of up to 55 km/h (34 mph). Most of them have a large, curved fin in the middle of the back which helps to stabilize them. The largest of the dolphins is the killer whale, in which the fin can be up to 2 m (over 6 ft) in length.

Dolphins are thought to be among the most intelligent of animals. They seem to be friendly towards humans, and are some-times kept and trained to do tricks, to help underwater engineers or to take part in underwater warfare. In a few cases dolphins are hunted by humans. In others, they get caught accidentally in fishing nets.

Porpoises

The word porpoise is used slightly differently in some countries. In Britain it refers to some animals like small, rather plump dolphins with short faces. They do not always have a back fin, but if it is present it is usually small and triangular, rather than backwardly curved. They have up to 80 teeth in their mouths, but these are flat or spade-shaped, not pointed. In America the word porpoise is used to include some of the small dolphins as well.

The common or harbour porpoise gets its name because it often swims near to land, although in the western Atlantic it migrates to deeper water during the winter months. At sea, it is usually seen in small groups, called schools, cartwheeling through the surface water to breathe about four times a minute. It can dive to over 50 m (160 ft), though its average time below water is only about four minutes. Dall's porpoise is more playful than the other porpoises and is said to be the fastest swimmer of all of the whales, reaching speeds of 50 km/h (30 mph) over short distances. Both species feed on small, non-spiny fishes such as herring. Large numbers of both species are killed each year, caught in fishermen's nets or hunted as food.

▼ Porpoises differ from dolphins in a number of ways: they are generally smaller with rounded rather than beaky faces and, whereas dolphins have pointed teeth, porpoises have squared teeth.

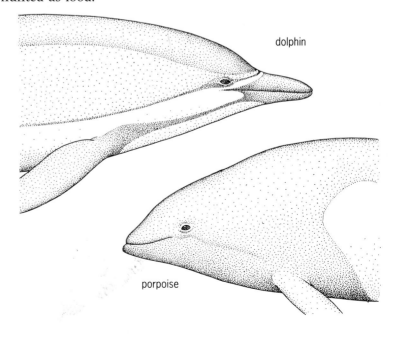

dolphin

porpoise

Seals

► Grey seal cow greeting her pup. The pup still has its creamy-white lanugo (birth coat) which it will shed after 2–3 weeks. Its new coat will resemble that of the adult.

Distribution
Mainly in cold waters of the northern and southern oceans. A few species found in warmer places, and one in Lake Baykal

Largest
Elephant seal: males up to 4·9 m in length; weight up to 2,400 kg. Females much smaller. (A greater difference in size between males and females than in any other mammal.)

Smallest
Ringed seal: length 117 cm, weight up to 45 kg

Number of young 1

Lifespan
Up to 40 years in the wild. Enemies include large sharks, killer whales, leopard seals, polar bears, and most important, humans.

► The walrus uses its huge tusks (up to 1 m long in males) to dislodge clams and other shellfish on the sea-bed. It then gathers them with its mobile, whiskery lips.

Seals and their relatives the sea lions and walruses are mammals whose four walking limbs are replaced with flippers, which make them slow and clumsy on dry land. But once they have slipped into the water, they are transformed. Their bodies are streamlined, and far more flexible than those of land mammals, so that they can twist and turn with amazing speed and grace as they play or chase after their prey.

Most seals hunt fish. A few kinds feed on krill, and walruses eat shellfish and sea urchins. Seals can hunt in murky or dark water. The whiskers round their faces can detect the changes in water pressure as something swims past. Even blind seals can feed.

Seals can remain in the water, even in polar regions, for long periods. Beneath their skin they have a thick coat of special fat called blubber, which helps to keep them warm. When they dive they are able to close their nostrils and their ears. Some species can stay below the surface for over 30 minutes and can go to depths of over 600 m (2,000 ft). As they dive, they breathe out and hold their breath, at the same time slowing their heart rate to 4–15 beats per minute, so that the oxygen in their blood is used up more slowly.

Seals come ashore to produce their young on islands or isolated beaches which are traditional breeding places. Seal's milk is over half fat, so the calf's growth is rapid. Females mate soon after the birth, and may leave the calf before it is three weeks old.

Toothless mammals

Anteaters

Anteaters feed on ants and termites and sometimes other sorts of insects, such as beetle grubs. An anteater uses the long claws on its front feet to tear open the nests of its prey. Its wormlike tongue is covered with tiny backward-pointing spines which are made gummy with sticky saliva. There is no escape for the scurrying insects, and a giant anteater (whose tongue is over 60 cm/24 in long) may mop up as many as 30,000 in a day.

Giant anteaters live on the ground, travelling slowly by day or night through the damp forests and savannahs. They are usually alone, although babies stay with their mothers for up to two years, often riding on their backs.

Other species of anteaters live in trees. They have prehensile tails which help them to climb and hold on securely. The smallest of them, the silky anteater, lives mainly in silk cotton trees. It rarely comes to the ground, and is difficult to see because it looks like a newly opened silk cotton pod.

Other kinds of animals also rely on ants and termites for their food. Spiny anteaters from Australia and pangolins from Africa and tropical Asia have large claws and long, sticky tongues like the anteaters of South America, although they are not related.

Armadillos

The name armadillo means 'little armoured one'. All armadillos are shielded with plates of bone and horn set in the skin of their backs, heads and tails. When attacked some can curl up into a ball. Those which are not able to roll up defend themselves with the huge claws on their front feet. But they are not aggressive and whenever possible prefer to escape danger by burrowing.

▲ A giant anteater feeding at a termite mound.

Armadillos are slow-moving animals, mainly active at night, when they hunt for insects, worms and carrion. Some armadillos produce a single young one each year, but most have a litter of identical cubs, all developed from a single fertilized egg. Most species of armadillos are now rare, partly because they have been hunted for food, and partly because of the destruction of their habitat.

Sloths

Sloths are upside-down animals, hanging with huge, curved claws from the branches of tropical trees. They can eat, sleep, mate and give birth in this position and very rarely descend to the ground, where they are nearly helpless. There are two groups of sloths; those with two toes on their front feet, and those with three. They look similar, but it is thought that they are not closely related.

Sloths have long coarse hair which is grooved. Tiny plants live in the grooves. They give the sloth a greenish tinge, which acts as a camouflage. Special insects feed on these plants.

Distribution
All of South America, Central America, and some parts of North America

Largest
Giant anteater: head and body length up to 120 cm; tail up to 90 cm; weight up to 39 kg

Largest armadillo
Giant armadillo: head and body length up to 100 cm; tail length about 50 cm; weight up to 60 kg

Smallest
Fairy armadillo: head and body length up to 15 cm; tail about 2·5 cm

Number of young
1 for anteaters and sloths, up to 12 for armadillos

Lifespan
About 12 years in the wild.

Spiny mammals

Distribution
Much of Europe, Asia, Africa, The Americas, Australia and New Guinea

Largest
Crested porcupine, up to 83 cm in length; up to 27 kg in weight

Smallest
Lesser hedgehog tenrec, about 10 cm in length

▼ The prehensile-tailed porcupine lives in Central and South America. It spends most of its time in trees, only coming down to the ground to eat.

Several unrelated groups of mammals have evolved spines as a means of protection from predators. Spiny mammals include porcupines, hedgehogs, some species of tenrec (a small mammal found in Madagascar), and the echidnas, also called spiny anteaters.

Hedgehogs

It is easy to recognize a hedgehog with its coat of more than 3,000 spines. These spines make the hedgehog fearless, for if it meets danger it can roll up into a prickly ball. Most natural enemies leave hedgehogs alone, but many are killed on roads where their spines are no protection against motor cars.

All animals have parasites, but the hedgehog's spines make it easy to see the fleas and ticks it carries.

Hedgehogs rest during the daytime. In the evening they set out and travel up to 2 km (over 1 mile) looking for food. They feed on insects, snails, slugs and grubs and the occasional frog or lizard, which they find mainly through their sense of smell. For their size, hedgehogs eat a very great deal. In the cold of winter when food is no longer plentiful they hibernate, making use of the fat stores built up in good weather.

Porcupines

Porcupines are armoured with sharp spines or quills, which cover most of their bodies. Some of the forest-living species of Africa and Asia, such as the brush-tailed porcupines, have long, but spineless tails which break easily. If they are attacked, the predator is left holding the end of the tail, while the porcupine escapes with its life.

The larger African and Asian porcupines have short tails, usually with very long quills, which they can rattle as a warning to predators. If this warning is ignored the porcupine will quickly back into its enemy. Its spines are very loosely attached and so will easily come off to be left in the predator's skin. The spines are not poisonous, but the wounds can become infected and kill predators, like lions and leopards.

American porcupines are tree-living. They are excellent climbers with large feet and long tails with which they cling tightly to branches.

Porcupines are mostly nocturnal animals. They have poor eyesight but good senses of hearing and smell. They feed on many kinds of plants, and in some parts of the world damage crops and trees. Also African porcupines carry fleas which can spread bubonic plague.

Rabbits and hares

Rabbits and hares are found throughout the world, having been introduced by people into many areas where they were not found naturally. They can survive in very different habitats: there is the snowshoe hare in the Arctic, the South American forest rabbit in tropical rainforest and the antelope jack rabbit in the Mexican desert.

Rabbits

Rabbits are gnawing animals, feeding on plants and usually living in groups and sheltering in burrows. When they feed they do not move far from home, so that a short dash can take them to safety. They rely on their good eyesight and senses of hearing and smell to warn them of enemies. They are hunted by many predators, including human beings. Baby rabbits are helpless at birth. Most kinds of rabbits produce a large number of young in the course of a year.

As a result, in places where they have no natural enemies, as in Australia, they can become pests and do a great deal of damage. In some ways rabbits and hares are like rodents, but there are many differences. One is that rabbits have four upper incisor teeth. There are two tiny ones behind the big incisors that you can see. These are completely covered with enamel, unlike the incisors of rodents, which have enamel only on the outer side.

Hares

Hares are so similar to their close relatives, the rabbits, that in some parts of the world creatures that should be called hares are known as rabbits.

In general, hares are larger, with much bigger ears, but the most important differences are in their ways of life. Unlike rabbits, hares live alone, usually in grassy places. They do not dig burrows, but make a shallow trench called a form, to shelter

in. A hare lies quite still when a dog or a fox approaches. It does not move until the enemy is very near. Then it leaps away. It can run very fast, zigzagging and jumping high, so that it can still watch its enemy. Hares also leap and chase each other during the mating season.

Baby hares are called leverets. They are open-eyed, furry and able to be active within minutes of being born. Their mother hides them near to her form for a few days and feeds them every evening, but they are soon able to look after themselves.

▲ Baby rabbits in their nest at eight days old. They already have some fur but their eyes will not open for another two days.

Distribution
Virtually worldwide

Largest
European hare, up to 76 cm in length and 5 kg in weight

Smallest
Pygmy rabbit, about 25 cm in length and 0·3 kg in weight

Number of young
Hares 2–4, rabbits up to 12

Lifespan
Up to 10 years in captivity, much less in the wild

◀ The black-tailed jackrabbit is not a rabbit but a hare. Its enormous ears help it to control its temperature in the hot desert where it lives.

Rodents

Rodents include rats and mice, guinea pigs, porcupines and squirrels. Almost half of all of the known kinds of mammals are rodents. They are sometimes called the gnawing animals, for in the front of their mouths they have only two incisor teeth in the upper jaw and two in the lower jaw.

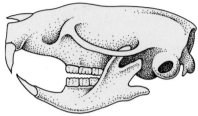

▶ **Rat (rodent)**
Rodents have long incisors with sharp edges, like chisels, for gnawing.

These are different from the incisors of most other mammals, as rodent incisors continue to grow throughout the animal's life. But they do not just get longer and longer. They are worn down by the tough plant food that rodents eat, and so they stay the same length. The incisors have enamel on the front only, and so the front is worn down more slowly than the back. This means the teeth are continually being sharpened to a razor's edge.

▶ **The majority of rats, such as this slender-tailed cloud rat, are forest-living animals which feed on seeds and leaves.**

▼ **The brown rat's intelligence and sharp senses of hearing and smell enable it to survive alongside humans, in spite of all efforts to exterminate it.**

Rats

The rat family is a huge one, containing over a thousand different kinds of small-sized rodents including mice, voles, hamsters and gerbils. Most species of rat have little contact with human beings, but the black rat and the brown rat have become major pests.

The black rat came originally from south-east Asia. It is a good climber, but needs warmth and so is most successful in the tropics. The brown rat from much further north, probably China, can stand cold weather. It is found in cities all round the world, and can even live in sewers. Rats are found wherever there are people. Both species of rat eat almost anything and often foul more than they eat. Both can carry diseases, some of which may be transmitted to human beings or domestic animals.

Squirrels

Unlike most small mammals, squirrels are active during the day-time. Their eyesight is better than that of other rodents and they are able to judge distances very well as they climb and leap in trees.

Tree squirrels feed on nuts and fruits and sometimes gnaw at trees to get at the sap. Like many rodents, squirrels store surplus food, usually by burying it. They forget where they make their larders, but they have a good sense of smell and are able to find nuts even under 10 cm (4 in) of soil. Tree squirrels make secure nests in hollow trees and also dens among the branches. These are called dreys.

Flying squirrels are small relatives of the tree squirrels. They are able to glide rather than fly, but they can steer to avoid branches. They also have many relatives which burrow. These are called the ground squirrels and include prairie dogs.

Dormice

Dormice are small, plump, furry-tailed rodents. They have long whiskers and large eyes, which are often made to look even bigger by a ring of dark fur. They are good climbers and usually live in woodlands or rocky places.

Dormouse means 'sleep mouse', for most dormice hibernate, in a deep sleep which may last for more than six months in a cold winter. Dormice snooze during the day, coming out of their nests at night to feed on seeds, nuts and fruit as well as insects and spiders. One species, the edible or fat dormouse, was kept by the Romans for food.

Voles

Voles may be mistaken for mice, but differ in having short tails and faces with small eyes and ears. They often feed on very tough plants. To deal with this, most voles have teeth which continue to grow throughout their lives, keeping pace with the wear caused by such a harsh diet. Voles rarely live for more than one year, but most females produce several litters of young in this time. Most are eaten by foxes, owls or other predators but sometimes

enough survive to cause a huge increase in numbers. They live in northern parts of the world.

Some northern voles are known as lemmings. These animals often have huge increases in population, which then crash to a low level again.

CARE OF PET RODENTS

Many species of rodents are commonly kept as pets. The most popular species include rats, mice, gerbils, hamsters and guinea pigs. All of these make excellent pets being very cheap to buy and to keep; taking up little space, and demanding a relatively small amount of attention. Most rodents will tame easily if acquired when very young.

An old fish tank, with a lid makes an ideal home for your pet as it is easy to clean, keeps out draughts and keeps in sawdust! Most rodents will need a layer of sawdust in their home, though gerbils will prefer a fairly thick layer of sand and earth in which they can burrow, and guinea pigs should have some straw.

Fresh water and food should be available at all times and your pet should have its sawdust and bedding (shredded paper is ideal) changed once a week.

Perhaps the only drawback to keeping rodents as pets is their short life-span. Mice live for only about a year, and the more long-lived pet species for only about three years.

◀ The bank vole is a common species over most of Europe and Asia. Like most voles it is often active during the daytime. It lives among rough vegetation or burrows in the surface of the soil. It makes stores of food, sometimes hiding its larder in an old bird's nest.

Distribution
Worldwide

Largest
The capybara: head and body length up to 134 cm; shoulder height 62 cm; weight up to 66 kg

Smallest
Pygmy mouse: head and body length may be as little as 4·5 cm and weight as little as 2·5 g. There are many other mice which are only very slightly larger.

Number of young
Variable, but several in most litters. Many species produce a series of litters through the summer.

Lifespan
Up to 20 years in beavers and marmots, but very short in most small species. Wild mice rarely survive for much more than a year.

◀ African porcupine family at the entrance to their burrow, in the Kalahari Desert.

Marsupials

▼ Marsupials are very varied in their appearances and their lifestyles. The Tasmanian wolf has not been seen since 1936 so it is almost certainly now extinct.

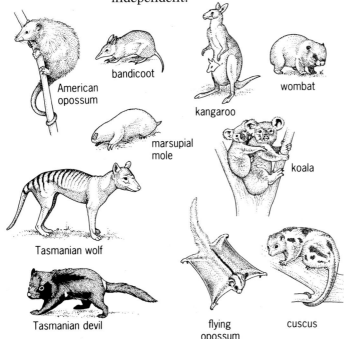

American opossum

bandicoot

kangaroo

wombat

marsupial mole

koala

Tasmanian wolf

Tasmanian devil

flying opossum

cuscus

Marsupials are sometimes called 'pouched mammals', as many female marsupials have a furry pouch on the underside of their bodies. Its function is to hold and protect the young from the time of their birth until they are strong enough to be independent.

Baby marsupials grow inside their mothers' bodies for only about six weeks, often less. When they are born they have hardly begun to develop and are very tiny. The largest is only about 2 cm (¾ in) long, and some are as small as a grain of rice. But they all have big forelimbs with strong claws with which to crawl through their mother's fur to her pouch. Once inside, the newborn finds a teat. This swells in its mouth, so it is fastened to its food supply. At first it is so weak that it cannot suck, but the mother pumps the milk into its mouth. Baby marsupials grow fairly slowly in the pouch.

Marsupial mammals are found mainly in Australia, New Guinea and South America. The reason for this is that for much of the last 100 million years Australia and South America have been island continents, cut off from the rest of the world. When Australia became separated from the other continents, almost the only mammals living there were marsupials, and in South America the mammals which were carnivores (flesh eaters) were marsupial. In both of these continents the marsupials evolved into many different sorts of animals, living in many ways.

About 10 million years ago when South America became joined to North America the marsupials had to compete with other mammals better suited to survive. Many became extinct, and we have only their fossil bones to show what extraordinary creatures they were. Australia has remained a separate island, so the marsupials there are still very varied. We can find grazing, climbing, burrowing, and flesh-eating marsupials, similar in their ways of life to the mammals of other parts of the world.

Distribution
Australia, New Guinea, South America, one species in North America

Largest
Red kangaroo: males may measure over 2·5 m total length, and weigh up to 90 kg; females are smaller.

Smallest
Pilbra ningaui: head and body length of adult may be as little as 4·6 cm, though the tail is as long again. Weight may be no more than 2 g.

Number of young
1 in most species; up to 18 for the opossums

Lifespan
About 10 years, less for the smaller species

Kangaroos

Kangaroos are marsupials that normally produce only one young at a time. At birth, a big red kangaroo is only about 2 cm (¾ in) long and weighs 0·75 g (¹⁄₄₀ oz). The joey (baby kangaroo) crawls to its mother's pouch and feeds and grows there for about eight months. It continues to take milk from her until it is about a year old.

All kangaroos have powerful back legs and long, narrow hind feet. They sit up on these, partly supported by their strong tail when resting. If feeding, or moving at slow speeds, they drop onto all fours, and when moving fast they hop.

Kangaroos are mainly active at night. The larger species are grazing animals feeding mainly on grasses. They often live in dry areas and can go for long periods without drinking. The small species, called rat kangaroos, eat many sorts of plants and fungi, and sometimes even include insects or worms in their diet.

Koalas

Koalas are climbing marsupials, living among the branches of eucalyptus forests in Australia. They generally sleep for about eighteen hours a day and are mainly active in the evening. They feed almost entirely on the young leaves and shoots of the eucalyptus trees they live in. These contain a great deal of moisture, so koalas rarely need to leave the trees to look for water. Their name comes from an Australian Aboriginal word which means 'the animal that does not drink'. Eucalyptus leaves contain strong-smelling oils and other chemicals which are poisonous but koalas have a very long gut which deals with these. In spite of this, they have a distinct smell of eucalyptus oil!

▲ When it first leaves the pouch a baby koala travels on its mother's back. By the age of eighteen months it will find a territory of its own.

Opossums

Some opossum species have pouches in which the young develop as kangaroos do, but many types do not. Most opossums live in forests and have naked, scaly tails which they use to cling to branches as they climb about. They feed mainly on small animals, including insects.

The Virginia opossum pretends to be dead if it is caught, or badly frightened. The Virginia opossum does this so well that its enemy often loses interest and the opossum escapes.

◄ Eastern grey kangaroo with joey in pouch. These kangaroos are able to graze during the day because they are large and feed in groups.

▼ Grey four-eyed opossum with young. The young leave the pouch after about 70 days, and are able to breed at the age of six months.

Egg-laying mammals

There are two families of mammals which lay soft-shelled eggs: the echidnas and the platypus. The development within the egg is very brief, and in all other aspects, the monotremes as they are called, resemble other mammals.

▶ **Short-beaked echidna foraging for ants. Echidnas are only active at midday during cold periods. When it is hot they feed at night or at dawn or dusk.**

Distribution
Australia, Tasmania and New Guinea

Largest
Long-beaked echidna, up to 90cm long; up to 10 kg in weight

Smallest
Platypus, about 50 cm long; about 1·5 kg in weight

Number of young 1–2

Lifespan
Echidna: up to 49 years in captivity (not known in wild) platypus: about 10 years in the wild, more in captivity

Echidna

The echidna is also known as the spiny anteater because it has a spiny coat, which protects it from predators. When alarmed the echidna curls up into a ball or, if it is on soft soil, it will dig rapidly down so that in seconds, only its spines are visible.

The female echidna has a pouch, into which she lays her single egg. The egg

hatches after 10 days and the young will remain in the pouch until its spines begin growing. As in other mammals, the young feeds on its mother's milk. Milk is produced by milk patches as echidnas have no teats. The young sucks the milk as it trickles through its mother's fur.

When not breeding echidnas live alone. They feed mainly on ants and termites and shelter in hollow logs or under thick vegetation. Breeding females dig a short burrow.

Platypus

When a platypus skin arrived in Britain in 1798 everyone thought it was a hoax. It took nearly 200 years before this strange little animal was accepted as a proper mammal. Not only does the platypus lay eggs, but it is also poisonous. Male platypuses have a horny spur behind the rear ankle which can be used, by way of a sharp kick, to deliver an injection of poison to an attacker. Enough poison is released to kill a dog.

The platypus lays two eggs in a special breeding burrow. When the young hatch she will feed them with milk. Platypuses are found close to water as they feed almost entirely on small water creatures, in particular insect larvae.

▶ **The platypus is well adapted for life under-water. It has a streamlined body, covered in thick fur which helps it maintain its body temperature, and large webbed front feet for propelling itself forward.**

Bats

Bats are the only mammals that have wings and are capable of true flight. Many are grotesque-looking animals with huge ears and strange faces. They produce high-pitched sounds which bounce off nearby objects. This 'echo' is picked up by the bat's large ears and the bat uses it to locate its prey and avoid obstacles. This is called echolocation.

Almost a quarter of all mammal species alive in the world today are bats. Nearly all are nocturnal (active only at night). Most eat insects, but some feed on larger creatures such as mice, or other bats. A few catch fish, and three species take blood from large birds or mammals. Some bats feed on nectar and are important in carrying pollen from flower to flower, while others are fruit eaters.

Most bats fly more slowly than birds, but have more control. They can turn, twist and fly without hesitation, through small gaps that would defeat the majority of birds. Flight uses a lot of energy. Most bats conserve their resources by letting their temperatures drop and remaining still when they are not flying. In cool parts of the

world bats hibernate, but a few species migrate to where there are better supplies of food.

There are still huge populations of many sorts of bats, but others are becoming rare, as a result of pollution and changes in the environment.

◀ **Mouse-eared bat. A bat's wings are made of a double membrane about 0·3 mm thick. When it is not being used for flying, the wing contracts between the supporting bones, so that it does not impede the bat's movements.**

Distribution
Throughout the world, except for the coldest areas and a few remote islands

Largest
Flying fox: head and body length over 40 cm; wingspan up to 2 m; weight up to 1·6 kg

Smallest
Kitti's hog-nosed bat: head and body length about 3 cm; wingspan 15 cm; weight about 2 g

Number of young
1, in most cases

Lifespan
Up to 20 years, even in small species

◀ **Fruit bats do not navigate by echo location. Instead they use their excellent eyesight. This female and her young are roosting in a tree. Only large fruit bats roost in such open spaces.**

Birds

Birds are warm-blooded animals which evolved from dinosaur-like reptiles millions of years ago. There are about 8,700 species of birds living in the world today.

All birds have wings and lay eggs. They are the only creatures to grow feathers. Birds have evolved a highly specialized body which enables them to fly efficiently. A few, such as the kiwi, have lost the power of flight.

Largest wing-span
Wandering albatross, up to 4 m. Albatrosses can sometimes glide for hours without needing to beat their wings.

Cruising speeds of birds
Mallard
 65 km/h (40 mph)
Pheasant
 54 km/h (34 mph)
Wandering albatross
 54 km/h (34 mph)
Dunlin
 47 km/h (29 mph)
Grey heron
 43 km/h (27 mph)
Herring gull
 40 km/h (25 mph)
Swallow
 32 km/h (20 mph)

Longest migration
Arctic tern, up to 40,000 km (25,000 miles) in a year. They return to the same mates and nest sites, of previous years.

Largest bird
Ostrich, 2·75 m high and weighs 150 kg. Males are larger than females.

Longest non-stop flight by small bird
Greenland wheatear, 4,100 km (2,500 miles). As insect-eaters they need to winter in a warm climate.

Fastest bird
Peregrine, 180 km/h (112 mph). It kills its prey as it hits it in mid-air.

Smallest bird
Bee hummingbird, 6 cm from bill-tip to tail

World of birds

Birds live in all parts of the world. Rain-forests, deserts, the open oceans and even the icy wastes of Antarctica are home for some birds. Up in the sky, swans may migrate at a height of 8 km (5 miles). Under the water, penguins may swim to a depth of 265 m (870 ft).

The variety of birds is amazing. There are birds which eat only plants and others which eat only fresh meat. Most hunt by day but some hunt only after dark. The ostrich grows to be taller than us, while the bee hummingbird would fit in the palm of your hand. Male birds are usually larger and often more colourful than the females; in many species they look alike. In just a few the female is larger or brighter.

Some species are great travellers. Wheatears are only a little larger than sparrows, yet each year some fly non-stop from Greenland to North Africa.

Different diets

Like all animals, birds need to find food to survive. To avoid competing for the same food many species have specialized diets and different ways of feeding. Humming-birds have long, thin, pointed bills to reach into flowers and feed on the nectar. Many wading birds have long, strong bills for probing the mud in search of worms or shellfish. Birds of prey have hooked bills for tearing meat. Ducks have flattened bills for

long-billed curlew

pelican's pouched bill

flamingo filter-feeding

hawfinch cracking cherry stone

eagle tearing meat

▲ Birds' bills are useful tools for feeding and some are highly specialized.

filtering water or mud. Sparrows have short, strong bills for cracking seeds.

Some fish-eaters such as herons, have long legs for wading; others such as cormorants, have shorter legs and webbed feet to help them swim, dive and chase fish under water.

Swifts spend most of their lives in the air. Their feet are very strong and their tiny claws allow them to cling to a rock but they are useless on the ground.

FLIGHT FOR SURVIVAL

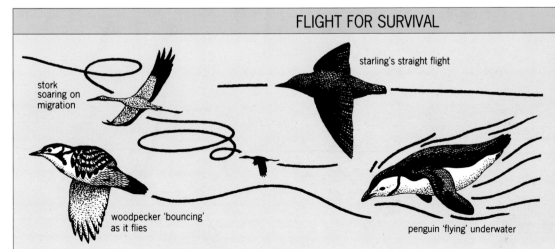

stork soaring on migration

starling's straight flight

woodpecker 'bouncing' as it flies

penguin 'flying' underwater

Most birds can fly. Even ground-living birds, such as pheasants, will fly into trees for safety. Not all birds fly in the same way. Starlings fly straight, moving their wings all the time and forming a star shape in the air. Woodpeckers close their wings between flaps and 'bound' along, moving up and down in the air. Penguins cannot fly like other birds, but they use their wings as flippers and 'fly' under water.

Garden birds

Many people enjoy watching birds in their gardens, and if we put out the correct food in the winter months they can be attracted close to our windows. A bird table, on a tall post that cats cannot reach, is a safe place for birds to feed. Throughout the year, make sure that the birds have a shallow dish of water to drink from. They may even take a bath in it!

The species of birds that visit your garden will depend a lot on whereabouts you live in the world, and even within a country. In winter, in the British Isles, the most common garden birds are sparrows, starlings, blackbirds, chaffinches, blue tits, great tits, song thrushes, greenfinches, robins and dunnocks.

▼ Unsalted peanuts or a coconut can be suspended from the bird table for those species which like to feed on hanging food, and for perching birds put out cheese rinds, cooked potato, seeds, berries, and bread and cake crumbs. During the warmer months birds should not be fed as they can find plenty of insects, seeds and other food during these months.
Put out water too, but remember to keep it free from ice during winter.

Watching birds

Beginning bird-watching is simple. Use a bird identification book and find out the names of your garden birds. Try to discover which are males and which are females, and watch how different birds behave.

If you have a local park with a lake, arrange a visit with some friends or your parents, because water birds are generally quite easy to identify.

Always wear dull-coloured clothes and try to move slowly so that you do not frighten the birds. You will need a notebook and pencil to record what you see. If you want to look at the birds more closely you will need binoculars (those marked 8x30 or 8x40 are best).

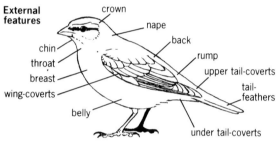

External features

crown
nape
chin
throat
back
breast
rump
wing-coverts
upper tail-coverts
belly
tail-feathers
under tail-coverts

Travelling around the world

Many animals, including birds, migrate: they move from one place to another and return again in a different season.

While some birds will not travel far from where they hatch, others, especially those breeding in the northern hemisphere, will

great tit

blackbird

greenfinch

robin

dunnock

chaffinch

song thrush

house sparrow

blue tit

starling

fly south for hundreds or thousands of kilometres to spend the winter in warmer, food-rich places.

Sometimes only part of a population will migrate, often those living farthest north or in the most mountainous regions. Mountain birds may travel only a few kilometres to lower levels to find food and a warmer environment.

The migrations of small birds are astounding. The tiny ruby-throated hummingbird migrates from North to South America, and this journey includes an 800 km (500 mile) crossing of the Gulf of Mexico. The British swallow crosses the Equator to winter in South Africa.

Sea birds make even greater journeys. Some go out to sea and spend the winter out of the sight of land. Arctic terns fly from their Arctic breeding grounds to winter in the Southern Ocean, sometimes reaching the coasts of Antarctica. They can cover a distance of 40,000 km (25,000 miles) in one year.

Birds in a changing world

Life is tough for birds. When young they must learn to find food and shelter, to survive extreme weather and avoid enemies. Even so, most of them will die in their first year. Although nature appears cruel, if all the birds survived, many of them would not be able to find enough food, so a balance is created. Unfortunately, we have the power to upset that balance.

The dodo was a victim of our interference. It was a huge, flightless pigeon which lived on the island of Mauritius in the Indian Ocean. Visiting sailors killed many of them for food, and the cats, pigs and monkeys which the sailors brought to the island destroyed the dodos' eggs. By 1670 all the dodos were dead. They had become an extinct species. Since then the great auk, the passenger pigeon and many other birds, especially those of the tropics, have also become extinct as a result of our influence.

The rapid growth of the human population and the huge demand for natural materials

predators, such as birds of prey, catch many birds

bad weather causes migrants to get lost

hunters kill millions of migrant birds

swallows must cross the Sahara Desert

they must find food as they fly

◄ Swallows, like other birds which migrate, face many dangers on their journey.

The Arctic tern migrates further than any other bird, travelling 17,000 km (11,000 miles) between its breeding ground in the Arctic and its winter home in the Antarctic. Because of this it sees more daylight in a year than any other bird.

Oldest wild birds known
Oystercatcher 36 years
Royal albatross 35·9 years
Osprey 31·2 years
Mallard 29 years
Fulmar 23 years
Mute swan 22 years
Swift 21·1 years
Starling 20 years
Swallow 16 years
Cardinal 13·5 years
Robin 12·9 years
The lifespan of birds varies between species.

have resulted in the destruction of many of the places where birds live. Marshes are drained to make farmland, forests are cleared for timber or for space to grow crops, and deserts increase in size because of over-grazing by domesticated animals.

Birds are also hunted as a sport by some people, but they are becoming increasingly protected by laws throughout the world. However, around the Mediterranean over 100 million migrating birds are shot or trapped by hunters each year, and unless the numbers of birds killed are controlled, even more species may become extinct.

Perching birds

When you want to identify different species of birds it often helps to know how scientists group them. Then it is easier to find the right section in a bird book. The order (group) with the largest number of species (over 4,000) is the Passeriformes, which really means 'sparrow-like'. They are usually called song birds or perching birds. All have four toes, three pointing forwards and one backwards, and you can often identify them by their calls and songs.

The most common garden birds, such as sparrows, blackbirds and robins, belong to this order. So do the tiny wrens and huge ravens, dull-coloured larks and brilliant birds of paradise. There are weavers which construct the most amazing nests, dippers which can walk under water, those great travellers the swallows and many more different species. In fact, about half the species of birds belong to this order.

Tit
Long-tailed tits feed on insects and seeds. They live in woods and open country.

Sandmartin
Sandmartins are insect-eaters nesting in colonies in sandy riverbanks and quarries.

Swallow
Swallows are insect-eaters. They feed in mid-flight.

Dipper
Dippers feed on the larvae of aquatic insects and are found near fast-flowing streams.

Nuthatch
Nuthatches feed on nuts and are found in woodland.

Yellowhammer
Yellowhammers are seed-eaters found in open scrub country.

Bullfinch
Finches feed on seeds, buds, fruit and insects. They live in fields and hedgerows.

Nightingale
Nightingales are insect-eaters living in thick undergrowth and woodland.

Whitethroat
Whitethroats eat insects and fruit and live in open woodland.

Wren
Wrens are small insect-eaters, usually found living in bushes.

Mistle thrush
Thrushes feed on a variety of fruits, insects, snails and worms, and usually live where there are trees.

Fieldfare
Fieldfares feed on fruit and insects. They nest in colonies in wooded areas.

Pied wagtail
Wagtails are insect-eaters and are typically found near running water and in moist grassland.

Skylark
Larks feed on insects and seeds. They live in open country.

Song birds

Most of the perching birds are song birds. They use songs and calls to communicate with each other. Birds sing by pushing air out through their open mouths.

Bird song has a number of different functions. Male birds may sing to defend their territories. Their song warns other males not to approach, but it may also serve to attract females. Females in their turn will sing a greeting song so that the male will know not to attack. Young birds sing to let their parents know they are hungry, and their parents will sing to warn them of danger, or to gather them together if they stray.

◀ **Lesser bird of paradise. All male birds of paradise have beautifully coloured plumage, very different to their closest relatives the crows.**

NEST-BUILDING

Most perching birds live in trees or bushes, and produce young that are quite helpless when first hatched. They must build sturdy nests to keep first their eggs, then their fledglings safe.

The materials used in nest-building vary with the size of the bird. Quite large birds such as rooks use twigs that are not easily blown away. Smaller birds use twigs or grasses. Some, such as the European black-bird, add mud to bind the nest together. Even smaller birds may use spider or insect silk to bind their nests together.

One type of perching bird, the rufous oven bird of South America, builds a solid two-roomed, enclosed nest made of a mixture of sand and cow dung, baked hard in the sun.

Birds of paradise

Birds of paradise are some of the world's most exotic birds because their feathers are brilliantly coloured and fantastically shaped. They live mostly in the wet forests in the mountains of New Guinea or on nearby islands. But four species are found in north-east Australia. When explorers first brought skins of these birds to Europe, people marvelled at them and thought they must have come from paradise because they were so beautiful.

Female birds of paradise are dull coloured, it is only the males that have the magnificent plumage. They use feathers to attract the females in elaborate courtship displays which are accompanied by unusual 'songs'. Their songs may be soft or loud. Some can sound 'mechanical' and others sound loud and explosive, rather like gun-fire.

Bird of paradise feathers have been used in ceremonial costumes by local tribes in New Guinea. During the last century many of the birds were shot for a plumage trade which exported their feathers to Europe and North America for ladies' hats.

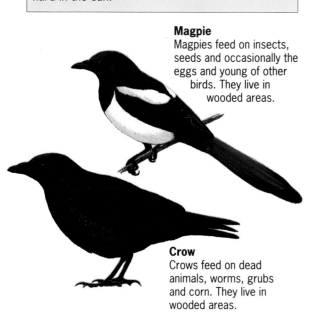

Magpie
Magpies feed on insects, seeds and occasionally the eggs and young of other birds. They live in wooded areas.

Crow
Crows feed on dead animals, worms, grubs and corn. They live in wooded areas.

Distribution
Virtually worldwide

Largest
Superb lyrebird, up to 1 m in length (including tail); weight up to 1·2 kg

Smallest
Short-tailed pygmy-tyrant; 6 cm long; weight 5 g.

Sea birds

▶ Pelicans' huge bills are used to catch fish. When pushed into water the lower bill expands forming a pouch which fills with water and fish. As the pelican lifts its head from the water the pouch contracts, forcing out the water, leaving the fish.

A Manx shearwater ringed in Wales was found in Brazil 16 days later. Minimum speed 740 km (460 miles) per day.

Arctic terns migrate from the Arctic to the Antarctic and back each year, a distance of about 35,000 km (22,000 miles) each way.

▼ Puffins produce single young, raised in nests built in shallow burrows in the softer soil of cliffs and islands.

Almost three-quarters of the Earth's surface is covered by sea. The oceans are as rich in food as the land and it is not surprising that birds take advantage of this food supply. But the open sea can be a harsh place for a bird and there are few safe nesting-sites. To survive and breed, sea birds must be very specially adapted, and that is why only 300 or so of the 8,700 species of birds have come to depend on the sea.

All at sea

Ornithologists have divided sea birds into several distinct groups (orders). The penguins are all flightless and live south of the Equator. They find their food by diving and hunting fish under water.

Albatrosses and shearwaters are great ocean travellers. The curious shape of their bill gives this group its name, 'the tubenoses'.

Pelicans are related to cormorants, gannets, boobies and frigate birds. Methods of finding food vary from the gannets' plunge-diving to the frigate birds' robbing other birds.

Gulls are a very successful group and many benefit from people by eating our rubbish. Their close relatives the terns feed mainly on fish, and because of this they have not increased in numbers like some of the gulls.

Auks, a group which includes the puffin, belong to the same order as the gulls. They nest in huge colonies on inaccessible sea-cliffs. Even before they are fully grown the young will fly from their cliffs and disappear out to sea for almost a year.

Skuas normally hunt by following other sea birds and then chasing and harrying them until they drop any fish they have caught.

Other sea birds

Birds such as geese cross the sea on migration, but they are not sea birds. Others, such as mallards, sometimes visit the sea in winter. But there are other ducks, such as eiders, which are generally found around coasts and may be called sea-ducks.

The phalaropes are wading birds, but two of the three species become sea birds when not breeding and live in the open ocean, usually out of sight of land for up to nine months. They find their food on the sea's surface.

Wading birds

Birds that feed in wet places need to be specially equipped. Long legs allow them to wade into water, and long bills help them to pick up small creatures, even those hiding in mud.

Herons are large with long necks, legs and toes for climbing in trees and among waterside plants. They eat animals, often fish, which they grasp in their dagger-like bills. Shorebirds spend much of the year near water. Many are at home in open spaces and breed on the northern tundra.

Size and feeding methods vary. Snipe have extremely long, straight bills and probe deep into the mud for worms. Oystercatchers have long, strong bills for prising open mussels, clams and other shellfish.

Avocets have long up-swept bills which they sweep from side to side as they search for tiny creatures to eat. Plovers have short, stubby bills. They run, stop, bend and seize their prey from the surface.

Flight for survival

Many waders, or shorebirds, live in the far north where food is plentiful in summer. The summer is short, but there is very little darkness and the young grow fast. Before the Arctic winter returns the birds must fly south. For some, like the ringed plover, which breeds over a wide area, the most northerly breeding birds make the longest journeys and winter farthest south. They 'leap-frog' the southerly breeding birds, which move hardly any distance.

Family groups do not migrate together. Often one parent leaves when the chicks are still young. If food is short this action may help the young survive. With some species, such as the redshank, the female leaves and the male looks after the young. On migration often the juveniles will form their own flocks.

Some waders make remarkable journeys. The lesser golden plover flies from Siberia to Australia and New Zealand. Others near by in Arctic Canada winter in South America and fly the shortest route, which is mostly over sea, a continuous journey of 3,800 km (2,400 miles).

Safety in numbers

Outside the breeding season many of these species form large flocks. They feed on estuaries where food is plentiful, and numbers may build up to thousands. As they search for food they all spread out over the mud. As the tide comes in they are driven off their feeding grounds and onto high-tide roosts where they wait, saving their energy, until the tide starts to fall again.

In Britain most 'waders' are sandpipers and their relatives. In North America these are called 'shorebirds', and 'waders' means herons and egrets.

Distribution
The world's oceans

Largest
Great black-headed gull, up to 78 cm in length; weight up to 18.7 kg

Smallest
Least sandpiper, 11 cm in length; weight 23 g

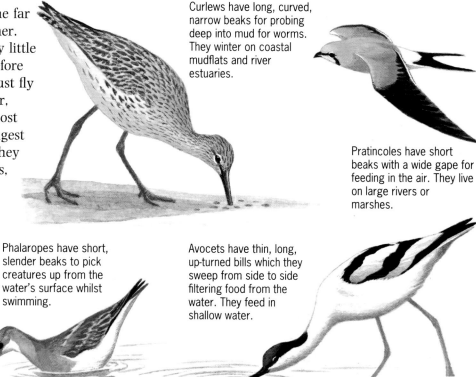

Curlews have long, curved, narrow beaks for probing deep into mud for worms. They winter on coastal mudflats and river estuaries.

Pratincoles have short beaks with a wide gape for feeding in the air. They live on large rivers or marshes.

Turnstones have stubby bills which they use to turn over stones and seaweed in search of food.

Phalaropes have short, slender beaks to pick creatures up from the water's surface whilst swimming.

Avocets have thin, long, up-turned bills which they sweep from side to side filtering food from the water. They feed in shallow water.

Wildfowl

Wildfowl is the name we often give to the large group of birds which include ducks, geese and swans. They are usually found near water and have webbed feet, short legs and tails, and long necks.

Ducks

There are several groups of ducks. Dabbling ducks, such as mallards, filter the surface water to find food. Diving ducks, such as pochards, search below the surface for vegetable matter. Perching ducks, such as mandarins, both perch and nest in trees. Ducks like eiders are called sea-ducks because they dive around sea coasts. Sawbills, like the mergansers, also dive for food. They have pointed bills with sharp, tooth-like edges for catching fish.

Stiff-tails are found in most parts of the world. Their stiff tail feathers can be raised or lowered and they often feed after dark.

There is also a group called shelduck which are neither true geese nor true ducks. Most are found south of the Equator, where they take the place of geese.

Geese

Unlike ducks, geese often pair for life and families keep together throughout the young birds' first winter. True geese are found only in the northern hemisphere. They graze on grass and other vegetation. At night they often roost on open water. Much of the year is spent in large flocks and many undertake long migrations.

Geese fall into two groups, 'grey geese', such as the greylag, and 'black geese', such as the Canada goose.

Swans

Swans feed on grass and water plants. They do not usually breed until they are 4 or 5 years old. Once pairs of swans are formed they tend to remain loyal for life.

Several species of swans are long-distance migrants, for example Bewick's swans fly from the Russian tundra to north-west Europe for the winter.

Distribution
Worldwide, except Antarctica

Largest
Trumpeter swan, up to 150 cm long and weighing up to 12 kg

Smallest
Indian pygmy goose, about 30 cm long, weighing about 185 g

Number of young
3–15 eggs depending on species

Lifespan
Up to 20 years, usually much less

brent goose

shoveller

mallard

goosander

tufted duck

▲ **Different species of wildfowl have different ways of finding food: grazing on the bank (brent goose); filtering the surface water (shoveller); up-ending in deeper water (mallard); diving to the bottom in deep water (tufted duck); or chasing and catching fish (goosander).**

Game birds

Lady Amherst's pheasant

golden pheasant

peacock

common pheasant

Throughout history birds have been hunted for food or sport. Those more commonly hunted in Europe and North America are pheasants, partridges and grouse, which are often called game birds. Bustards, quails and some wading birds, such as snipe and woodcock, are also traditionally game birds, as are turkeys and guineafowl in some parts of the world.

Pheasants

Members of the pheasant family are heavy, ground-living birds with short, rounded wings and strong feet and claws for scratching at the soil to find food. Many will fly into trees and bushes to sleep safe from predators at night. There are pheasants, or their relatives, in most parts of the world.

The family includes the partridges and the tiny quails, some of which make amazingly long migrations. Peacocks and jungle fowl are close relatives of the true pheasants.

Jungle fowl

Scientists believe that the red jungle fowl is the ancestor of our domestic fowl or chicken. It is a forest bird which lives wild in south-east Asia. Like other pheasants it has horny 'spurs' on its legs which it uses when defending its territory. Jungle fowl have been domesticated since the 5th century BC and possibly even earlier.

Grouse

Some grouse are found in dense forests, others on snowy mountain tops. Those species that live on mountains or in the north are often called ptarmigan. They moult into a white winter plumage for camouflage in the snow.

All male grouse defend territories they have chosen. Some have elaborate displays which often take place at leks, 'dancing grounds' where males strut around showing off to females.

▲ Pheasants and their relatives have some of the most attractive and exotic feathers in the bird world.

Distribution
Virtually world-wide

Largest
Blue peafowl, up to 2·3 m in length; weight 3·8 kg

Smallest
Asian blue quail, length 14 cm; weight 43 g

The largest feathers in the world belong to the crested argus, a pheasant with tail feathers over 15 cm wide and 150 cm long.

Birds of prey

▶ The golden eagle has a wingspan of up to 2·2 m. It hunts by sight, feeding mainly on small mammals.

Distribution
Virtually worldwide

Largest
Andean condor: length 116 cm; weight 14 kg

Smallest
Black-legged falconet: length 14 cm; weight 35 kg

▼ Vultures gorge on the muscle and body organs of a carcass. Hundreds may gather together at a time.

This name could refer to any bird which hunts and kills, even a robin catching a worm. But usually when we talk of birds of prey we mean falcons, hawks and vultures. Often owls are included, though they are not related to the others.

Birds of prey are so called because they prey on and eat other birds, mammals, fish, reptiles, insects, worms and also dead creatures. All have hooked bills, powerful feet with sharp talons, and big eyes. Their sight is better than ours and they have good hearing.

Out to kill

Hunting methods and types of prey vary enormously. Honey buzzards that eat bees have blunt talons for digging out bees' nests. Their faces are covered with stiff feathers as protection against stings. Fish eagles dive feet first into water. Vultures soar, searching for signs of a dead animal. Vultures are unusual birds of prey because they are scavengers that rarely kill.

Lammergeyers drop bones onto rocks to get at the marrow. Harriers fly low over the ground searching for small mammals and

birds. Sparrowhawks have long legs for grasping prey. They also have short, broad wings and long tails for manœuvring in the woods which they inhabit.

Peregrines use their speed in flight to hunt other birds. Red-footed falcons use their feet to catch large insects in flight. Ospreys have water-proofed plumage, and nostrils which close as they dive into water after fish.

Hunters hunted

For years we have hunted down birds of prey. They have been shot, trapped and poisoned to protect game birds from being hunted by them. Many have been taken into captivity for falconry. The use of chemicals in the countryside between 1950 and 1980 was also harmful to birds of prey and many populations declined rapidly as a result of poisoning.

Owls have soft plumage to help them fly quietly, and a large head with forward-facing eyes to help them judge distances. Around the eyes is a facial disc which helps to direct sound into their large efficient ears. One of the toes can be brought round so that four talons grip prey from four different directions.

Owls can see in very poor light, and their hearing is so good that they can locate their prey in darkness. Most species do need some light before they are able to hunt, but barn owls have such exceptional hearing they are able to catch prey in total darkness. Owls catch prey with their feet. Small prey is swallowed whole, and larger prey is torn up with the bill. Once or twice a day owls regurgitate a pellet of material they cannot digest, such as bones, fur and parts of insects.

▼ Barn owls usually live alone or in pairs. They roost in farm buildings, hollow trees or caves. They feed on small rodents and birds.

Falconry

This ancient sport uses trained birds of prey to hunt wild birds and other animals. It may have originated in China 4,000 years ago.

The sport was common in Europe in the Middle Ages. It almost died out in the last century, but has recently been revived. Hawks, falcons, eagles and buzzards are the most commonly kept species. Once all were taken from the wild. Now more and more are bred in captivity.

Owls

Owls are generally thought of as the nocturnal (night-time) birds of prey, but not all owls hunt at night. Short-eared owls, for instance, hunt by day, but most owls are well equipped for night hunting.

Parrots

Distribution
Mainly in Southern
hemisphere

Largest
The hyacinth macaw,
about 100 cm from bill to
tail

Smallest
The buff-faced pygmy
parrot, 8·4 cm in length

Strangest
The kakapo of New
Zealand, which is nocturnal
and flightless

There are more than 300 different species of parrots in the world. Most are brightly coloured and very noisy. All parrots have a very curved bill, a short neck and short legs. Their toes are arranged so that two toes point forwards and two backwards. Males and females usually look very similar.

Some species of parrots are in danger of extinction because tropical forests are being cut down and also because of the number of parrots being sent to Europe and North America as pets.

Most parrots eat only vegetable matter, including seeds, berries and nuts. Some eat pollen, nectar and insects as well. Often parrots hold their food in the foot while they are feeding. The tongues of most parrots are short, thick and fleshy, and help the bird to hold a seed or nut in the top part of its bill while it cracks the nut with the lower part.

The kea, which is a parrot living in New Zealand, has evolved some of the habits of a bird of prey. It looks 'buzzard-like' and its long, hooked bill is used for tearing flesh. It feeds mainly on dead creatures, but it is accused of killing sheep.

Most parrots live in the tropics, especially in lowland forests, but some live in mountain regions and others are at home in cooler areas.

Talking birds

How some birds, such as parrots and budgerigars, manage to imitate human speech puzzles scientists, because monkeys, which have a similar vocal arrangement to humans are unable to copy the human voice.

It seems that some birds may learn to talk in the same way as human babies. They become strongly attached to a person and copy sounds they hear, although they probably do not understand what they are saying. They are likely to continue developing the sounds if it gains them attention.

▶ **The yellow-headed Amazon parrot is, like most parrots, vegetarian. It is popular as a pet because it can be taught to talk. Because of the pet trade and the destruction of their environments many species of parrots are near extinction.**

The oldest of all birds may have been a sulphur-crested cockatoo, called 'Cocky Bennett', which lived in captivity in Australia and is claimed to have been 120 years old when it died.

Hummingbirds

◄ As it hovers to suck nectar, the wings of this Rivoli's hummingbird beat so fast they have become a blur.

Distribution
Eighty-eight species are found in South America. The rest are in North America or the Caribbean.

Largest
Giant hummingbird, length 21.5 cm

Smallest
Bee hummingbird, length 6 cm

Hummingbirds will hover when feeding, beating their wings at more than 70 times a second, making a humming sound.

All hummingbirds feed on nectar. Many have long, specially adapted bills and tongues for reaching deep into different flowers. The plants often need the hummingbirds, because pollen rubbed off onto the birds' feathers, is taken from flower to flower and helps the plants reproduce. Hummingbirds also eat insects and spiders.

There are two ways of feeding. Either the bird chooses an area where there are enough flowers to supply it with food and then it defends this territory, or it travels round visiting different flowers. Generally the male is more colourful than the female. Because their bodies are small, their wing-beats fast and their temperature high, they need a lot of energy and they must feed frequently. If the temperature falls they become torpid, rather like a very short hibernation, and so save energy.

Small is beautiful

Most hummingbirds are very small. The bee hummingbird from Cuba is under 6 cm (2¼ in) from bill-tip to tail-tip and is the smallest bird in the world. The largest, the giant hummingbird, is only about 20 cm (7¾ in) long.

Female hummingbirds make tiny nests and lay just two white eggs. Depending on the species the nest may be built on a twig, slung under a leaf or constructed in a cave. In most species the male takes no part in rearing young.

Migration

A few hummingbirds migrate to find food and avoid cold weather. The ruby-throated hummingbird flies from eastern North America as far as Panama, and the journey includes an 800 km (500 mile) non-stop flight across the Gulf of Mexico. The rufous hummingbird travels 3,500 km (2,000 miles) from Alaska to Mexico.

▼ A hummingbird's wings are unlike those of almost all other birds. They can move freely in all directions from the shoulder, enabling the bird to hover while holding its head quite still. It also means hummingbirds can fly backwards!

Flightless birds

Distribution
Antarctic coasts (penguins), Africa (ostriches), New Zealand (kiwis)

Largest
Ostrich 2·75 m high, weighing up to 150 kg

Smallest
Little spotted kiwi 35 cm long, weighing 1·2 kg

▼ **The ostrich must remain on guard against predators.**

All the flightless birds in the world today are probably descended from ancestors which were able to fly.

Flightless birds may be water birds or land birds. Many of them live on islands. They are able to feed and breed without needing to fly. They escape any enemies by diving if they are water birds, and hiding or running away if they are land birds. It is a sad fact that many flightless birds have become extinct, especially those living on islands, because they have not been able to survive the arrival of people, their animals and the changes they have made to the environment.

Ostriches

At a maximum height of 2·75 m (9 ft) ostriches are too big to fly. Instead they have powerful legs for running and, at speed, they use their wings for balance. When frightened by a predator an ostrich will sprint away from danger at 70 km/h (44 mph). The ostrich is also the only bird to have two toes on each foot, most birds have four. As with horses the number of toes has been reduced by evolution to increase running speeds.

Kiwis

Three species of kiwi live in New Zealand, and are all not only flightless, but have almost lost their wings altogether. Kiwis live in burrows in forests and only come out at night. In this way they avoid a number of predators.

▼ **North Island kiwi scratching for insects and worms.**

◄ Emperor penguins travelling across an icesheet. They are able to move faster on their stomachs, 'tobogganing' along.

Penguins

Penguins are flightless sea birds which live south of the Equator. Because of the position of their short legs, they usually stand upright and travel rather slowly on land. If they need to travel faster they lie on their bellies and 'toboggan' along. In water, however, their streamlined bodies and flipper-like wings help them to shoot along like small torpedoes.

A life in the water

The sixteen species of penguins alive today look rather alike. Most have dark blue or grey backs and white fronts. Both males and females look alike. Young penguins are covered in grey or brown down.

Penguins are heavy and this helps them to dive. Emperor penguins can stay under water for nine minutes or more and may reach a depth of 265 m (870 ft).

Those penguins which feed near the shore or in deep water are mostly hunting fish. Some species eat squid and others have a staple diet of a common shrimp called krill.

Life on ice?

The cold continent of Antarctica may seem a harsh place for a bird, but for emperor and Adelie penguins it is home, and both breed and feed around its coasts. Gentoo, chinstrap and macaroni penguins nest on Antarctica, outside the Antarctic Circle, on the land closest to South America. Other species nest on sub-Antarctic islands, Australia, New Zealand, South Africa and the southern tip of South America.

Emperor of the ice

The emperor penguin is the largest penguin, standing over 1 m (39 in) tall. It nests farther south than any other penguin and lays its eggs at the start of the Antarctic winter, which means it lives through some of the worst weather conditions experienced by any bird.

Temperatures may fall to below –40°C (–40°F). Wind may reach hurricane force. Snow continually blows, and there is no food. Males incubate the eggs on their feet, hidden under folds of skin for 60 days or more. During this time females are away feeding. The incubating males huddle together for protection from the weather.

When the young hatch, the males will have lost almost half their body-weight, but by then the females will have returned to help the males feed the young. On average only one out of five emperor penguin chicks will survive.

Migration
We still do not know much about the migration of penguins. Those in warm or tropical climates do not migrate, but many of those breeding farther south move north as winter approaches.

▼ All penguins are mainly black and white, but size and head patterns differ greatly. The penguins are not drawn to scale.

emperor   Adelie   jackass   rock-hopper

Reptiles

▶ The tuatara, an ancient reptile that can reach 60 cm in length.

Crocodiles, snakes, tortoises and lizards all belong to this large class of animals, the reptiles. Reptiles have backbones and strong limbs, though they cannot move very fast for more than a short time. They use lungs to breathe air, and have a tough, dry and usually scaly skin. They are 'cold-blooded', which means they can only control their body temperature by moving into cold places when hot, and warm places when cold.

In the breeding season males use bright colours or dances to attract females. After mating, the females choose a sheltered place, or make a simple nest, where they lay a fairly small number of eggs. These usually have a papery shell, but are otherwise very much like birds' eggs. In most cases they are left to be hatched by the heat of the sun, but some reptiles remain near the nest, and a few kinds, such as crocodiles and some snakes, look after their eggs and young. The females of some reptiles, most of which live in cool parts of the world, hold the eggs inside their bodies until they are ready to hatch. The eggs are always laid on dry land, and the babies that hatch from them look just like their parents.

DIFFERENT KINDS OF REPTILES

In the past, many kinds of reptiles flourished. The dinosaurs, which were reptiles, included the largest known land-living creatures. Today there are only four surviving orders (groups) of reptiles:

Turtles and tortoises are all armoured with a bony shell. Many swim well and live in water, but must come onto land to lay their eggs. Tortoises feed almost entirely on vegetation but some turtle species are flesh-eaters.

Rhynchocephalia contains one living species, the tuatara, which lives on a few islands off the coast of New Zealand. It is the only survivor of a big group of reptiles which were important during the days of the dinosaurs.

Lizards and snakes are the best-known and the most abundant reptiles. There are more than 6,000 species in all. Apart from the largest iguanas, lizards and snakes feed mostly on insects and other small animals.

Crocodiles and their relatives are the bulkiest of today's reptiles, and all live in or near water, although they have to come ashore to lay their eggs. All are flesh eaters.

Alligators and crocodiles

◄ Alligators swim by moving their long, powerful tails from side to side.

The members of the crocodile family, alligators, crocodiles, caymans and gavials, are the largest reptiles. Most are endangered because their skin is valued for leather and their habitats have been destroyed.

Alligators

True alligators seem to be able to survive in colder conditions than their relatives. They live further north and may hibernate during the winter. The Chinese alligator spends much time in a burrow dug into a river bank where its eggs are laid.

We know more about the American alligator than other alligators, as it is one of the most intensively studied of all reptiles. But probably other species of alligators live and develop in much the same way.

Crocodiles

Crocodiles are water-living, hunting reptiles. They belong to an ancient group of animals which has changed little since the days of the dinosaurs. They may seem harmless as they bask beside warm rivers or lakes or float, log-like, in the water, with only their nostrils and eyes above the surface. But they are far from harmless. When swimming, the thrust of their flattened, oar-like tails drives them fast towards their prey.

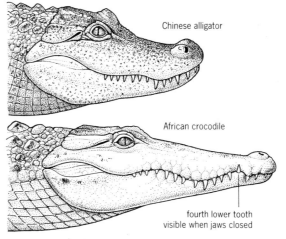

Chinese alligator

African crocodile

fourth lower tooth visible when jaws closed

Young crocodiles feed on insects, but for most of their lives fish is their main food. Their jaws are set with sharp pointed teeth, ideal for holding such slippery prey. Big, old crocodiles can tackle larger creatures and may even be a danger to humans and livestock.

Crocodiles are gentle mothers. After mating, a female makes a nest of mud and plant debris near the water's edge. Here she lays her eggs and stays on guard near by until they are ready to hatch. When they are ready the babies croak from inside their eggs and the mother helps them to escape. She gathers them into her huge mouth and carries them to the water. Here she continues to guard them, for they have many enemies, including their own father!

◄ Alligators have shorter, blunter snouts than crocodiles. When a crocodile's mouth is closed, the large tooth fourth from the centre on the lower jaw still shows near the front of the mouth and fits into a notch in the upper jaw. No lower teeth can be seen when an alligator shuts its mouth.

Distribution
Rivers, lakes and the edge of the sea in warm parts of the world

Largest
Some Nile and salt-water crocodiles may grow to over 6·5 m in length; up to 1·5 tonnes in weight

Smallest
West African dwarf crocodile, 1·5 m long

Number of eggs 25–95

Lifespan
Up to 100 years

Snakes and lizards

► Costa Rican eyelash viper. Vipers are poisonous snakes which lie in wait for prey to ambush. As the viper's fangs pierce its victim venom is injected into its body.

▼ Rock python eating a Thomson's gazelle. Snakes cannot chew their food but must swallow it whole. The snake can dislocate its jaws so it can move each part separately and work its prey into its mouth. Its scales stretch apart and its ribs spread as it swallows.

Most snakes move by throwing their bodies into curves which push against any unevenness of the ground. Snakes which move in this way are helpless on smooth surfaces. Snakes are so long and thin that their bodies are not wide enough for all the internal organs that other vertebrates have, so snakes have only one very long lung, instead of two.

In cool parts of the world snakes hibernate during winter. In spring they look for mates. Males often compete with each other or display to females. After mating, most female snakes lay eggs, although some do give birth to live young.

A snake can track its prey using its long, forked tongue which flickers over the ground, covering a wider area than a single pointed tongue could do. It picks up tiny traces of scent left by animals such as mice. Some snakes, like grass snakes, catch their prey by grabbing and swallowing it. Others, like pythons, loop their body round it and suffocate it by making it impossible for the animal to breathe.

SNAKE BITES

Vipers are front-fanged snakes. They have long hollow fangs at the front of the mouth.

Back-fanged snakes, like the boomslang, have large fangs towards the back of the mouth.

About one-third of all kinds of snakes use poison. This usually affects the nervous system, and paralyses the prey. It also helps to break down the food, so poisonous snakes digest their prey much more quickly than non-poisonous snakes. The poison glands are at the back of the upper jaw, and the poison is always injected into the prey by hollow or grooved teeth called fangs.

In the vipers and their relatives, the fang is like a hypodermic syringe which injects the poison. The fang is on a movable bone, which enables it to be folded away, for it is so large that the snake could not otherwise close its mouth.

Snakes cannot chew their food, as their teeth are like curved needles. Instead, they swallow it whole. A snake that has just swallowed a large meal will have a distinct bulge in its body. To take such a mouthful they must unhinge their lower jaws, at the centre and the sides. They can move each part of the jaw independently and so 'walk' their prey into their throats.

Snakes also use their poison to defend themselves, and can injure and sometimes kill large animals, including humans. Many people fear and dislike snakes, killing them whenever possible.

Lizards

Most lizards are small, agile creatures, which can be seen in the warmer parts of the world, sunning themselves or, warned by their sharp eyesight and good sense of hearing, scuttling away from danger.

◄ The collar of the frilled lizard may be as much as 25 cm in diameter. Normally it lies in folds close to the lizard's neck, but if the lizard is alarmed the collar is raised so the lizard has the appearance of being larger than it really is.

Some kinds of lizards are able to shed their tails if caught by a predator, and escape. The tail will grow again.

In general, lizards feed on insects or other small animals. Apart from geckos they have little contact with human beings.

Geckos have sticky pads on their feet and are able to climb walls or walk upside-down on ceilings. They are welcome in many houses, for they feed on flies and other household pests.

Lizards have different ways of life. A large number of species live in dry places. Some of these are burrowers, hunting grubs and other small prey underground. They 'swim' through the soil, using their bodies in a fish-like way. Generally their skin is silky smooth and their legs are tiny. In some cases, as in the slow-worms, they have no legs at all.

Distribution
Mostly in warm parts of the world

Largest snake
Anaconda, may grow up to 10 m in length

Smallest snake
Thread snake, less than 12 cm in length

Largest lizard
Komodo dragon grows to over 3 m long, weighs over 100 kg

Smallest lizard
Rhampholeon marshalli, 3·5 cm long

◄ An iguana from the Galapagos Islands. This large lizard (up to 1·2 m in length) feeds mainly on plants. It is becoming very rare.

Shelled reptiles

▼ Giant tortoises are found only on remote tropical islands. They were able to evolve to such a size because they were isolated from predators. Many are now extinct, and those remaining are protected.

Shelled reptiles include the land tortoises, the freshwater terrapins and the sea turtles. Their shell is made of horny plates covering bone. On the inside of this, their backbone, ribs and some other bones are attached. This makes them very stiff and slow-moving creatures.

largest turtles, the great sea turtles, feed on many sorts of marine plants and animals, including jellyfish. They spend most of their lives at sea, but during the breeding season they visit shallow water to mate, then at night the females come ashore to lay their eggs. They take most of the night to dig a pit and lay up to 200 eggs. These take about three months to hatch. The young turtles then dig their way out of the nest and go down to the sea. They have many predators, including humans, and large numbers are killed before they are old enough to breed.

Terrapins

Terrapins are a kind of turtle living in fresh water. They have flatter shells than their land-living cousins, the tortoises, so they can lie almost unseen on the bed of a pond or stream. They can hold their breath for a long time, and some species have pointed snouts so that they are barely visible when they come up for air.

They are flesh eaters. Some, like the alligator snapper, lie in wait for unwary fish or smaller creatures. It lies with its mouth open, and at the back of its tongue there is a small worm-like organ. If a fish tries to eat this 'worm', the snapper has an easy meal. Other species are hunters, some even being powerful and quick enough to catch ducks.

Tortoises

Distribution
Mostly warm parts of the world

Largest
Leathery turtle: measures over 2 m in length and weighs over 500 kg

Smallest
Common musk turtle, 8·3 cm in length

Lifespan
Giant tortoises at least 180 years

▶ One of the 90 species of living turtles and tortoises. Like the others this turtle has no teeth. Instead it has a strong horny beak with which it crushes insects and other invertebrates.

Tortoises are land-living armoured reptiles. They are well protected against enemies, but their domed shells are heavy, so they are slow-moving creatures. They protect themselves by pulling their heads, tails and legs into their shells. To breathe, tortoises must pump air into their lungs using special muscles since, like turtles, their shells stop their rib cages expanding.

At one time giant tortoises were found on many remote tropical islands. Unfortunately, most of these are now extinct, but the few that survive are carefully preserved. Many other species of tortoise are threatened by damage to the environment or hunting.

Turtles

All of the turtles have toothless jaws, edged with sharp bone to chop up their food. The

Amphibians

Amphibians are animals with backbones and, usually, a soft, moist skin. Their name comes from two Greek words, and means 'two (both) ways of life'. This is because most amphibians start their lives in water and later change so they are able to live on land.

Life history

Most amphibians mate in the water, which is where the females lay their eggs. They may lay up to several thousand eggs each year. The eggs are not protected by a shell, but soon after they are laid the outside swells to make a jelly-like surround. The eggs hatch quite quickly, but the baby that emerges is unlike its parents. Instead it resembles a little fish, with a big head and a wriggly tail. This is a tadpole. At first the tadpole breathes with gills and feeds on minute plants that live in the water. As it grows its body changes. It loses its gills and grows lungs and legs, so that it can live on land. Its diet changes too. Adult amphibians eat flesh, feeding on many sorts of small animals. This change in body and way of life is called a metamorphosis.

Although adult amphibians are able to live on land, they must keep moist. They have lungs but these are usually not very big, and so amphibians breathe through their skin as well. They can only do this if their skins are damp, so they rarely move far away from water.

Cold-blooded

Amphibians are 'cold-blooded' animals. This means that their body temperature depends on the warmth of the air or water in which they are living. When the weather is cold they become very sluggish, and in the cooler parts of the world, such as Britain, they hibernate in the winter months. Most kinds of amphibians live in warm countries.

Kinds of amphibians

There are three main kinds of amphibians. **Blind worms** are strange creatures found only in the tropics. Although they have backbones, they have no legs and look very much like worms. **Newts and salamanders** look like lizards. Some kinds, such as axolotls, can remain in the tadpole stage for all of their lives and live entirely in water. **Frogs and toads** have no tails, but usually have very long hind legs, which they use for jumping. Amphibians defend themselves by hiding during the daytime and being active mainly at night. They are also protected by poison glands in the skin.

Distribution
Mostly in warm countries

Largest amphibian
Japanese giant salamander, which grows to a length of 1·6 m

Smallest amphibian
One of the South American arrow poison frogs, which measures up to 1·3 cm

◄ Axolotls are the tadpoles of a certain type of salamander. They are unusual in that many axolotls remain tadpoles all their lives but are still able to breed

▼ Blind worms are unusual amphibians as only one species lives in water. All the others burrow underground and are rarely seen on the surface. Many do not even need water to breed.

Frogs and toads

Frogs and toads are amphibians (able to live in water and on land). They have long powerful hind legs for jumping. Many also have webbed feet for swimming and have large bulging eyes to help them spot prey.

▼ The colourful red-eyed leaf frog from the rainforests of Costa Rica.

Frogs

Adult frogs live on land and feed on worms and insects, which they catch with their long sticky tongues.

At a certain time of year, frogs travel to a pond to mate. The male frogs croak to attract the females. Some frogs have pouches under their throats which they can blow out to make a louder sound. Frogs mate and lay their eggs in water. The eggs (frog-spawn) hatch into tiny fish-like tadpoles, which gradually change shape, lose their tails and develop legs as they grow.

Most frogs match their background, so their enemies cannot see them easily. They have slime on their skin which can make them taste bad. Many frogs have poisonous flesh or skin. If an animal eats them, it will feel very ill, and will avoid eating frogs in future. Poisonous frogs often advertise the danger with bright yellow, orange, red and black patterns, so they are easy to avoid.

Distribution
Widespread in moist habitats throughout the tropical and temperate zones. They cannot live in salt water.

Largest
Goliath frog from West Africa measures 80 cm fully stretched out, and weighs 3 kg

Smallest
A Cuban frog measures only 8.5 mm

Most poisonous
Golden dart-poison frog from South America. One adult frog contains enough poison to kill 2,200 people.

Toads

Toads are tailless amphibians like their relatives the frogs, but with shorter, broader bodies, and warty skins. They go in water only to breed, returning every spring to the best places, using their excellent homing instincts. In some areas yearly toad watches are organized to protect breeding toads as they cross roads. In most toads the male attracts the female with a mating call.

Toads are most active at night, or during rainy spells, when they hunt worms, grubs and any insects that they can catch. Only moving prey attracts the toad's attention. It is caught on the toad's long tongue, which it flicks out and back into its mouth in less than one-tenth of a second. During hot dry spells toads burrow into the ground and become inactive. This is called aestivation.

▲ Poison from the arrow poison frogs of South America is used by local people to tip their arrows.

▼ This Kenyan leopard toad, like most toads, has very drab colouring making it difficult to see against its natural background.

METAMORPHOSIS

albumen   area of yolk

Egg
Frogs and toads may lay thousands of eggs. The eggs are protected by a jelly coat and vary in size and colour depending on species.

developing external gills

nostril

developing mouth

suckers

One day after hatching
Tadpoles are not completely developed when they hatch. At first they stay in one place attached by suckers. They use yolk inside their body for food.

fold of skin grows over external gills

hard, rough lips

Three weeks old
As the tadpole develops it is able to swim about to feed on water plants.

wider mouth

webbed foot of back leg

Two months old
The tadpole begins to develop legs. Its hind legs develop flrst. At this time the lungs also develop and the digestive system changes so the frog can eat small water animals.

remains of tail

Three months old
Finally the tadpole loses its gills and leaves the water as a small frog with a tail stump.

Adult
The tail stump is absorbed as the frog becomes an adult.

Fish

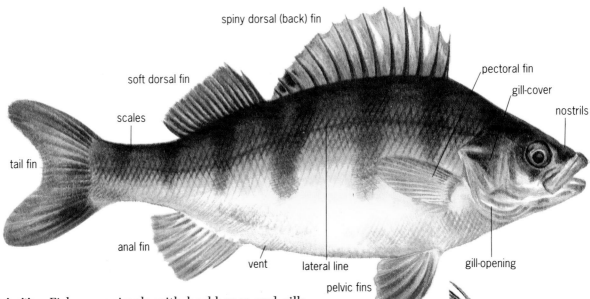

spiny dorsal (back) fin

soft dorsal fin

scales

tail fin

anal fin

vent

lateral line

pelvic fins

pectoral fin

gill-cover

nostrils

gill-opening

▲ Fish are covered with protective scales and are streamlined so they move easily through water. Their tail fin pushes them forwards, and the other fins are for steering and keeping upright.

Fish are animals with backbones and gills. They all live in water and may be found in unpolluted swamps, ponds, lakes and rivers. Some live in the cold and darkness of cave streams, and a few kinds can even survive in hot springs. But most fish live in the sea, especially in the shallows close to land, or in the surface waters of the ocean.

Sharks and their relatives are known as the cartilaginous fishes, and have a gristly skeleton. The rest, which are called the bony fishes, have a skeleton made of true bone. Most of them also have an armour of overlapping scales, which are made of very thin plates of bone.

Streamlined for swimming

Water is about 800 times as dense as air, so fish have to work hard to swim through it. Those that go fastest, like mackerel and tunny fish, are very streamlined, with a crescent-shaped tail. Slower-moving fish, like tench and carp, have deeper bodies and squarer tails. Fish living in coral reefs are usually very narrow from side to side. This probably helps them to find safety between the branches of coral. Some kinds of fish, like rays and turbot, live on the sea-bed. They have flattened, camouflaged bodies, and so are hard to see.

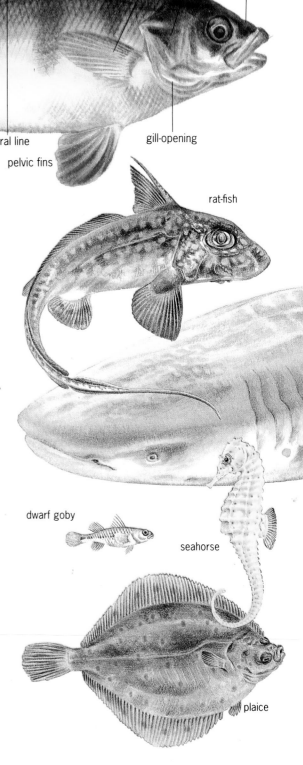

rat-fish

dwarf goby

seahorse

plaice

When they swim, most fish use powerful zigzag muscles which move their bodies and tails from side to side. Only a few kinds move by paddling with their fins. Fins are mainly used for balancing, stabilizing and braking.

Most kinds of fish have a swim bladder: a gas-filled bag which acts like an internal lifebelt and holds the fish up in the water. Watch a goldfish in a tank. It does not sink, even when it is totally still. When it wants to swim, all of its energy goes in to pushing itself forwards through the water.

Life cycle of a fish

A few kinds of fish are born alive, but most hatch from eggs. Usually there is a definite breeding season, which is triggered by the right temperature and amount of light.

Some fish, like eels and salmon, migrate long distances to reach the best place to spawn (produce eggs), but most fish are unable to move from sea water to fresh water.

The majority of fish species lay huge numbers of eggs. These are almost always fertilized outside the body of the female. It is unusual for fish to take any care of their young, although there are some kinds which produce smaller families and look after them. Among these it is often the male, rather than the female, that protects the babies until they are big enough to be independent.

Fish living in fresh water or near the sea-shore, usually lay eggs that sink to the bottom, where they may be hidden among plants. Open-sea species generally lay very tiny eggs which float. When these hatch they become part of the sea plankton. Very few of these tiny fish survive, as they provide food for many other animals.

As they grow, many kinds of fish live in schools, which contain fish of the same age and species. A school of fish behaves as a single unit. If danger threatens they swim close together, twisting and turning like one fish.

Largest fish
The whale shark, up to 18 m long, weighs over 40 tonnes

Heaviest bony fish
The ocean sunfish, nearly circular in shape, may measure 4 m long and weigh over 1,500 kg

Largest freshwater fish
Arapaima, up to 3 m long; weight up to 200 kg

Smallest fish
Pygmy goby, up to 11mm long; weight 4–5 mg

Lifespan
Unknown for big fish, although some sturgeon have lived over 80 years. Many fish live only about a year, or even less.

Fastest
Sailfish, about 109 km/h

whale shark

sailfish

◄ There are about 43,000 species of animals with backbones, and over half of these are fish. Some of the species that have evolved are very strange indeed.

porcupine fish

electric eel

Atlantic flying fish

Some kinds of fish do not live in schools, but occupy and defend territories. This can be seen in coral reefs, where a single head of coral will be defended by several fish. Some other species are territorial only during the breeding season. The male stickleback, for instance, protects a small area in which he makes a nest. He entices females to lay their eggs in it, and drives away all other males.

Most fish grow throughout their lives. In many fish it is possible to tell how old they are by looking at their scales, or at some

bones, called otoliths, in their ears. These grow at different speeds at different times of the year, so they form rings, like tree rings, which can be read to give the age of the fish.

The senses of fish

Fish have the same basic senses as we do: sight, hearing, touch, scent and taste. Most fish have eyes on the sides of their heads. This gives them all-round vision, which they need because a fish is unable to look behind by turning its head. Most fish see

▼ A school of blackbar soldierfish in the Caribbean.

best when they are looking forward, and many seem to be long-sighted when looking sideways. Many fish have good colour vision. This is important in the courtship of some species, and in the species which can change their colour to match their surroundings.

Fish do not have ears that they can twitch, for their ears are inside their skulls. Like those of other vertebrates, a fish's ears function as organs of balance as well as for hearing. Sounds travel very well under water, and many fish make noises to communicate with each other. Usually these are drumming or grunting notes, made by muscles which twang against the swim bladder.

Many fish live where there is not much light, and their sense of touch helps out their sense of sight. Some have finger-like projections called barbels round the mouth. With these the fish can explore the sea or river bed.

More important is the *lateral line system*. This is a series of very sensitive nerve endings lying just below the skin along the side of a fish. Any movement in the water makes underwater waves which cause changes of pressure in all directions. The lateral line system detects them, and the fish knows that there may be an enemy or a possible meal near by.

Most fish have a very good sense of smell. Many use it to find their prey. Some, if they are injured, release a special substance from their skin into the water. When other members of the school smell this, they are aware of the danger and swim quickly to safety. Salmon have another use for their sense of smell. They probably use their smell memory to migrate back to the stream where they were born to lay their eggs in the same place.

The sense of taste is related to the sense of smell. Most fish have taste buds in the mouth. Some species, such as the catfish and sturgeon, also have whisker-like barbels around the mouth. These barbels are used both to taste and touch.

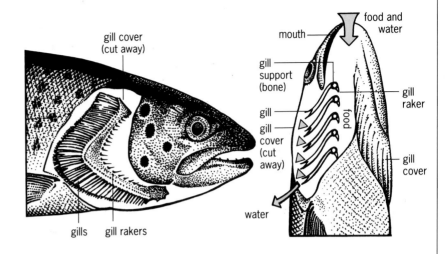

▲ Gill cover cut away to show gills and gill rakers. Gill rakers are like combs attached to the bone supporting each gill. They let water, but not food, pass out through the gills.

The food of fish

Freshwater fish eat all sorts of food including water plants, snails, worms, insects and their larvae, and other fish. Some fish, like grey mullet, are called detritus feeders. They suck up mud from the river bed and digest from it the huge numbers of tiny organisms living there. In the open sea, where there are no rooted

◄ Cleaner wrasse busy at work in the mouth of the fierce moray eel. The wrasse feeds on parasites on the skin of other fish, which in return do not harm it.

plants, most fish are flesh-eaters. Some feed on plankton and are called filter feeders. They take a mouthful of water and plankton, and push it out over the gills. The plankton is filtered out, and the fish then swallows it. This saves energy, as the fish uses the same action to breathe and feed. Even some very large fish, such as basking sharks, are filter feeders. Other species eat shrimps, squid, or other fish. Most deep sea fish have huge mouths and teeth and some can swallow creatures bigger than themselves. They have few chances to feed and may not eat again for months.

Oceans and seas

Life at the top

In the sunny surface waters of the oceans lives a floating community of billions of microscopic creatures, the plankton. Tiny algae use the Sun's energy to make their own food. They, in turn, are food for shrimps, prawns, and the young of many other sea animals including starfish, snails, crabs and barnacles.

Larger animals use the wind to drift across the sea. The Portuguese man-of-war and the by-the-wind-sailor, animals that look similar to jellyfish, have gas-filled floats to catch the wind. The bubble-raft snail produces a froth of bubbles as a float, while the sea slug *Glaucus* gulps in air.

The tiny animals in the plankton are transparent, and difficult to see in the sunlit waters. Larger animals, including fish, have blue backs and silvery bellies for camouflage. Hunting sea birds in the air above cannot see them against the blue of the sea, and larger fish in deeper water cannot easily see their silver bellies against the light of the sky.

Open ocean animals

The shallow waters near coasts provide shelter and nutrients for many different kinds of animals. Out in the open ocean there are fewer species, but many fish and a few large mammals like dolphins, porpoises and whales live here. Some, such as baleen whales, basking sharks, herrings and prawns, feed by filtering the water for plankton. Others, such as white sharks and barracuda, hunt fish. Squids, turtles and sea birds hunt here, too.

Life in the deep sea

In dimly lit waters, hunters can spot the silhouettes of their prey against the faint light above. Here, many fish have silvery scales along their sides to reflect any light

Going down

As you go down deeper in the ocean, the pressure of the water above increases sharply, making it difficult to move quickly. The temperature also falls to around 2°C (36°F) in deep water. The light intensity decreases, until at 1,000 m (3,000 ft) there is no light at all. In shallower water, the colour of the light changes with depth. Water absorbs red light more than blue, so below a certain depth only blue light remains, and the scenery appears blue.

around them and disguise their shapes. Others are flat-sided, with extremely narrow silhouettes. Some have rows of light-producing organs on their bellies to camouflage their shadows.

The deep ocean is a cold, dark world. Gulper eels and hatchetfish swim with their large mouths open to catch whatever they can. Some fish have elastic stomachs, to make the most of rare meals. The deep sea angler fish uses a luminous lure on its snout to attract prey. Lanternfish use light organs as flashlights to find prey. Other fish, shrimps and prawns use them to attract mates or confuse predators.

Many bottom-dwelling fish rely on smell and taste. They have long taste-sensitive fleshy whiskers, called barbels, which probe the mud for food. The rat-tail fish has a long tail lined with detectors to pick up vibrations from other fish. The tripod fish props itself above the mud on three fins to smell for prey.

Hatchetfish (above) and *Pseudoscopelus* (right). Many deep sea fish swim open-mouthed and can eat prey larger than themselves, because food is so rare and meals may be months apart.

◄ Cross section of a part of the ocean showing some of the creatures which live at different levels. The animals are not drawn to scale.

1 mollusc
2 worm
3 herrings
4 plankton
5 pelican
6 seaweeds
7 swordfish
8 flying fish
9 gulls
10 porpoise
11 basking shark
12 Portuguese man-of-war
13 jellyfish (*Rhizostoma*)
14 tuna
15 humpback whale
16 krill
17 seal
18 large blue shark
19 lanternfish
20 heteropods
21 sea gooseberries
22 hatchetfish
23 sperm whale
24 squids
25 octopus
26 mako shark
27 chaetognaths
28 prawns *(Nebalia)*
29 viperfish
30 swallower
31 anglerfish
32 lamp shell
33 rat-tail fish
34 brittlestars
35 glass sponge
36 tripod fish
37 crinoid
38 dead fish

Sharks

Sharks known to have attacked human beings include: great white shark, hammerhead shark, tiger shark, bull shark, porbeagle, mako shark, grey shark, great blue shark.

There are many different types of shark. Some, like the zebra horn shark, are sluggish bottom-dwellers which feed on shellfish. Others, like the whale shark and basking shark, are filter-feeders and eat plankton. However, the best-known sharks are the fast-swimming predators such as the great hammerhead, the mako and the great white. These sharks feed mainly on fish, though the great white also eats dolphins and seals.

Sharks, together with rays and skates, are different from other fish. Their skeleton is made entirely of cartilage rather than

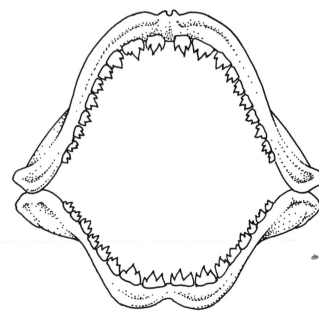

dorsal (back) fin

five gill slits

tail fin

claspers (male only)

Distribution
In oceans throughout the world but more common in warmer water

Largest
Whale shark, grows to a length of 15 m. (Largest shark in British waters is the basking shark, length 9 m.) Both of these species are plankton feeders.

Largest flesh-eating shark
Great white shark, grows to a length of 6 m

Smallest
Dwarf shark, 15 cm long

bone. Their skin is made of thousands of tooth-like structures known as 'placoid scales'. They give shark skin a texture like sandpaper.

The teeth in a shark's jaws are modified placoid scales and grow in rows. When a tooth is damaged it drops out and the next tooth behind moves forward to replace it. At any one time the shark may have up to 3,000 teeth in its mouth. The teeth may be pointed and serrated for sawing flesh or flattened for crushing shellfish.

▲ The jaws of a shark.

nostril

eye

teeth arranged in rows

fins that cannot fold up

electricity through a series of pits in their snout. This means they can detect the electrical charge produced by the nerves in an animal's body. Sharks are also able to see very well in dim light.

A completely new species of shark over 4·5 m (15 ft) long was described in 1983. It has been named the megamouth shark because of its huge mouth. It is a filter-feeder like the whale shark and eats shrimps and jellyfish. So far only three specimens have been caught.

There are fewer than 100 shark attacks upon humans every year. However, thousands of sharks are killed for food and liver oil. The 'rock salmon' used in fish and chip shops is a shark, the lesser spotted dogfish.

▼ The large scalloped hammerhead, like all hammerhead sharks, has its eyes on the outer edges of its 'hammer'. Hammer-heads have been known to attack humans.

Another way in which sharks differ from most other fish is that they do not have a swim bladder, a gas-filled organ, to keep them afloat. If they stop swimming they sink. Sharks produce very few eggs, and unusually for a fish, the eggs are not released, but fertilized within the female's body. In most shark species the eggs hatch within the female and she gives birth to live young. However, in some species, the eggs are protected by horny egg cases. The 'mermaid's purse' you may find on the seashore is the egg case of a shark, the dogfish.

Sharks have a keen sense of smell and can detect one part of blood in a million parts of water. They also sense vibrations produced by struggling fish. Shark fishermen in the Pacific islands rattle coconut shells under-water to attract them. All sharks can detect

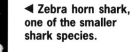
◄ Zebra horn shark, one of the smaller shark species.

Insects

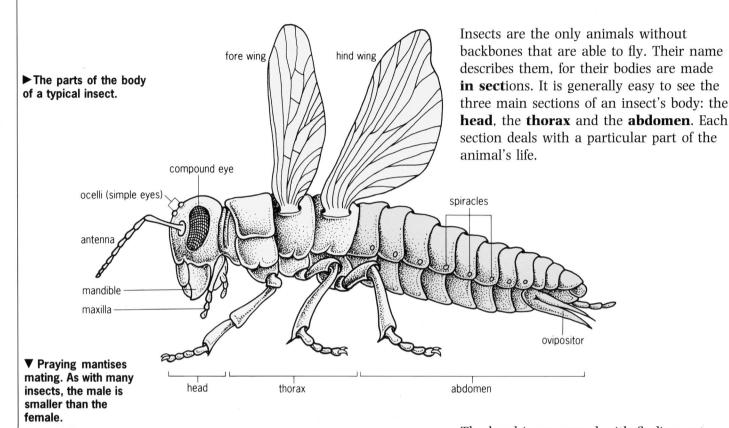

► **The parts of the body of a typical insect.**

fore wing

hind wing

ocelli (simple eyes)

compound eye

antenna

mandible

maxilla

spiracles

ovipositor

head   thorax   abdomen

▼ **Praying mantises mating. As with many insects, the male is smaller than the female.**

Insects are the only animals without backbones that are able to fly. Their name describes them, for their bodies are made **in sect**ions. It is generally easy to see the three main sections of an insect's body: the **head**, the **thorax** and the **abdomen**. Each section deals with a particular part of the animal's life.

The head is concerned with finding out about the world around it. The insect has a mouth, eyes and antennae (feelers), which are for smelling as well as for feeling, on its head. The thorax is concerned with movement. Most insects have three pairs of legs (some have only two) and most adult insects have two pairs of wings attached to the thorax. The main part of the gut and digestive system is in the abdomen and so are the sex organs. Insects may also store fat in the abdomen.

A skeleton on the outside

Like crabs and spiders to which they are related, insects' bodies are supported and protected by a hard outer armour, the exo-skeleton. This is waterproof and prevents them from drying up in the air, as may happen to some other small creatures. It enables insects to live almost everywhere in the world, even in deserts and on mountains, although few survive in the sea.

The great disadvantage of the exoskeleton is that it cannot stretch, so all insects get larger in a series of stages called moults. At certain times the hard exoskeleton splits and the insect, which has grown a new pliable skin beneath the old one, wriggles out. At first this new cover is soft and can expand to allow for growth. But it hardens quite quickly to protect and limit the insect once more.

There are more different kinds of insects than any other sort of animal. One reason for this is that all insects are small. Each kind of insect can live in a tiny part of the environment. Even a single tree may be home to lots of them. Some may live among the roots, some on the bark, some under the bark, some on the twigs and some on the leaves. Some may be active during the daytime, while others are active at night. Different kinds of insects are active at different times of the year. If we think of the environment as a cake, each kind of insect takes a very tiny slice, so very many of them can share it.

Feeding

Most insects feed on only one type of food and cannot change from it. But between them, insects can eat almost every sort of food. Because of this, some of them are pests of human crops and stores. Most, however, do no damage. Bees and butterflies pollinate flowers and crops and are useful to us. Ladybirds and some hoverflies feed on pests such as greenfly. We rarely think of the most important insects. These are the recyclers, such as beetles, which feed on the remains of dead plants and animals. As these remains pass through the insects, they are broken down into chemicals which fertilize the soil when returned to it. Plants can then make use of the minerals from things that have died, for new growth.

Distribution
Almost worldwide

Largest
Giant stick insect, 33 cm long

Heaviest
Goliath beetle, weight up to 100 g

Smallest
Fairy fly, 0·005 mg and just visible with the naked eye

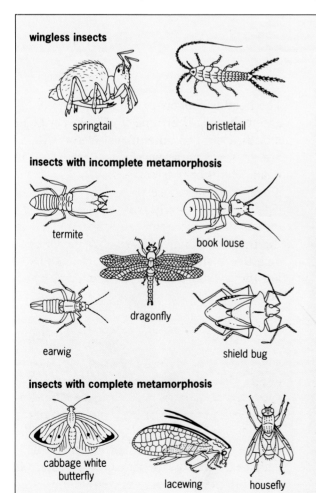

wingless insects

springtail

bristletail

insects with incomplete metamorphosis

termite

book louse

dragonfly

earwig

shield bug

insects with complete metamorphosis

cabbage white butterfly

lacewing

housefly

Wingless insects

It is likely that the first insects, which evolved more than 300 million years ago, had no wings, although their bodies were divided into three sections, like insects of today. A few kinds like this still survive. They are scavengers, and are common wherever there are dead leaves and plants, throughout the world. The young, when they hatch from the egg, look like tiny versions of the adults.

Incomplete metamorphosis

There are many kinds of insects with wings. Some, like grasshoppers and bugs, produce young which look like their parents, but at first have no wings. At each moult their wings get bigger. At last, when they are full grown, they are able to fly. As adults, they feed on the same food as they did before they were full grown. Insects like this are called exopterygote insects, insects with incomplete metamorphosis.

Complete metamorphosis

The third group of insects have young which hatch from their eggs as larvae (grubs). They look very different from their parents and they feed on different food. When they are full grown, they become pupae and change to the adult form, which is able to breed. Most of the adults feed chiefly on nectar, and are important as pollinators of flowers. Most familiar insects are insects with a complete metamorphosis. These are also called endopterygote insects.

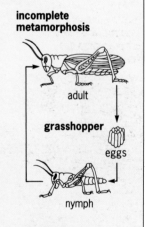

incomplete metamorphosis

adult

grasshopper

eggs

nymph

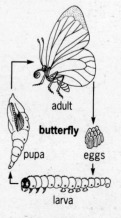

complete metamorphosis

adult

butterfly

pupa

eggs

larva

Butterflies

Distribution
In all but the coldest parts
of the world

Largest
Some of the birdwing
butterflies have a wing-
span of about 28 cm, as
does the Hercules moth.

Smallest
Johanssonia acetosea of
Britain, wingspan 2 mm

▼ Close-up of a
butterfly wing showing
the thousands of tiny
scales.

Butterflies are mostly brightly coloured,
day-flying insects. Their colours come from
thousands of tiny scales on their wings.
These maybe actually coloured, but in some
cases the surface of the scales causes light
to be broken, so the wings are iridescent
with rainbow colours, which change as the
insect moves. Often the undersides of the
wings are dull colours to camouflage the
butterfly when its wings are folded. This
protects it from birds and other predators.

Mating, eggs and caterpillars

Bright colours are very important to
butterflies. They find and court their mates
with a show of colour. Some butterflies also
use scent in their courtship; some of the
scales on the wings of the males have a
perfume which attracts the females. After
mating, female butterflies lay batches of
eggs on suitable food plants, but die soon
after and never see the caterpillars which
hatch from the eggs. The caterpillars feed
and grow, then they pupate. In the pupa
(chrysalis) the butterfly develops and then
emerges.

METAMORPHOSIS

Monarch caterpillar

Chrysalis of the monarch
caterpillar

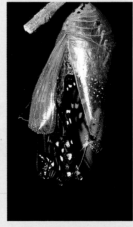

Emerging from the
chrysalis as a monarch
butterfly

Monarch butterfly

Moths

Moths, like butterflies, have wings which are covered with tiny scales. They often get trapped on window panes, and if you catch one to let it out you will find a fine dust on your fingers. This is made by some of the scales, which have brushed off as the moth fluttered.

There are far more moths than there are butterflies. Some are very tiny indeed, but some are even as big as the biggest butterfly. Although they are closely related to butterflies, moths generally lead a different way of life. They are mostly active at night. Because of this they tend to be drab in colour, unlike the brightly coloured butterflies, mostly active in the daytime. During the day they rest somewhere like on a tree trunk, where they are very hard to see because they are so well camouflaged.

◀ Unlike many butterflies this striking birdwing does not have drab outer-wing surfaces. Its bright green and black colours advertise its poisonousness.

▼ The giant atlas moth has a wingspan of up to 25 cm and lives in the rainforests of southeast Asia.

Brightly-coloured flowers can attract butterflies to feed. The butterfly unrolls its long, tubular tongue and sucks up the nectar which is hidden deep inside the cup of a flower. Some butterflies are also attracted to decaying corpses, or the droppings of animals, from which they suck the liquid.

Long-distance flights

All butterflies have four wings, but these work together like a single pair. A butterfly beats its wings fairly slowly: about twenty times a second for a cabbage white. Yet many butterflies can fly fast and powerfully. Even some of the smaller species travel long distances on migration. Comma butterflies, for instance, can fly from the central Sahara to Britain, a distance of about 2,000 miles, in fourteen days.

Moths have a very good sense of smell, which they use to find both their mates and their food. Many male moths have very elaborate antennae. These are the 'nose' of the moth, and are used mainly to smell out a suitable female. A male moth can follow the scent of a female across 18 km (11 miles) of country and town, ignoring all other sorts of smells.

Moths get most of the nectar they feed on from long-tubed, strong-smelling, pale-coloured flowers. Honeysuckle, jasmine and tobacco plants all provide food for moths.

Beetles and bugs

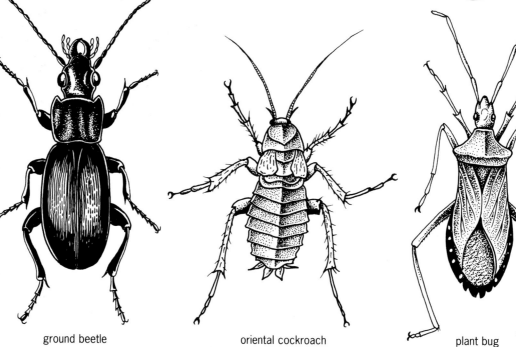

▶ Cockroaches and bugs look like beetles, but are different in several ways. A cockroach's head is partly hidden under the front of its body, and its front wings, if present, are not thick and hard like a beetle's. The front wings of a bug are thick and hard at the base, but are thin and papery at the tips.

▼ Adult seven-spotted ladybirds feeding on aphids. Ladybirds are often encouraged by gardeners as they eat large numbers of the pest aphids.

ground beetle   oriental cockroach   plant bug

There are more different kinds of beetles than any other sort of animal, and new species are being discovered all the time. They are found in every environment except the sea and on snowfields, and in every continent except Antarctica. Some eat flesh, especially that of other insects; others feed on plants, both living and dead. The goliath beetle is one of the largest of all insects and weighs more than a sparrow. Yet some of the smallest of all insects are also beetles, measuring less than 1 mm in length.

It is easy to recognize beetles, for unlike most other insects they have a heavily armoured look. This is because their front pair of wings, called elytra, have become thickened and are hinged back to cover the abdomen. Their hind wings are large and papery. When the beetle is on the ground they are folded and tucked away beneath the elytra. When a beetle flies the elytra are held upwards and forwards, for only the hind wings beat. The elytra give the beetle lift, rather like the wings on an aeroplane. The hind wings are rather like the plane's engine, providing the power for flight.

Eggs and grubs

Beetles start their life as an egg, usually laid in a place where there is plenty of food. A few species, like the sexton beetles, look after their young, but many parent beetles die before their eggs hatch. The creature that comes out of the egg is very different from the adult beetle. It is a larva (grub), soft-bodied unlike its parents, but with hard biting mouth parts, to help it feed and grow. Most beetle larvae complete their growth within a year, but some, feeding in dead wood in cold places, take much longer. The record is about 30 years, making these the longest-lived of all insects. When its growth is complete, the grub finds a safe place to pupate. During pupation, the large, fat body of the larva changes to form the adult beetle. This is called metamorphosis. Some adult beetles do not feed at all, but merely drink a little dew or nectar. This is because the grub has provided them with all the energy they need to mate and lay eggs.

Beetles, on the whole are not easy to find. This is because most of them dislike the light. They are either busy under fallen leaves, or among the roots of grasses, or simply hidden away during the daytime. Only a few, like the ladybirds, and some of the ground beetles, make themselves obvious. As these taste horrible they are safe from predators.

A few beetles are pests, feeding on crops or food stores, but many more are useful because they are recyclers, returning dead things to the soil so that plants can use them once more. Some feed off other pests, and so are useful to farmers and gardeners.

▲ Sexton beetle on animal corpse. It will bury the corpse and then lay its eggs in it. Later the grubs will feed on the decaying flesh.

Bugs

'Bugs' is a word used by many people when they want to talk about insects. But not all insects are bugs. True bugs all have one thing in common, despite varying greatly in size, shape and way of life. This common characteristic is their inability to eat solid food. All bugs have mouth parts which are like long, thin, sharp-tipped drinking straws. With these, bugs pierce the stems of plants to suck up the sap, or the skin of animals to drink blood.

Pond skaters and water boatmen are bugs that hunt other small animals. They are easy to see in ponds or slow-flowing streams. They are protected by having partly toughened wings. So are shield bugs, which are common on plants in summer. Some shield bugs are brightly coloured, a warning that they taste nasty.

Bugs can be pests. Many are agricultural pests. Greenfly and other aphids are probably the best known of these. But some, like the bed bug, attack humans, and can sometimes spread diseases.

The bombardier beetle protects itself by shooting jets of chemicals at attackers.

Distribution
Worldwide

Largest beetle
Goliath beetle: weight up to 100 g; length about 15 cm

Smallest beetle
A feather-wing beetle: length about 1 mm

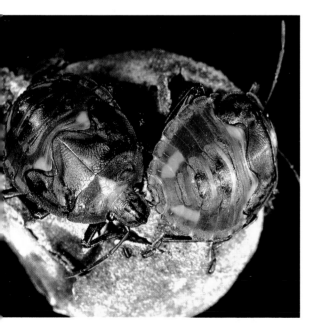

◀ Bugs do not have a complete metamorphosis as butterflies do, but develop gradually, although colour change can be dramatic. These are the young of the harlequin bug, and already look similar to the adult.

Flies

▶ Hoverflies are important pollinators as they feed on nectar.

Distribution
Worldwide

Largest
Mydas fly, body length 7·5 cm

Largest dragonfly
Wingspan about 35 cm. Some fossil dragonflies were much bigger, the largest had a wingspan of nearly 1 m.

Smallest fly
Midge, about 1·5 mm long

▼ The robber fly feeds on other insects. It has dagger-like mouthparts for piercing and sucking the blood of its prey, which can be insects as large as dragonflies, grasshoppers, bees and wasps.

Flies are among the commonest of insects, and many people think of them as being dirty and spreading disease. Although some are harmful to humans in this way, most are not. Flies live in a great variety of ways. Some of these seem to us to be unattractive, but even flies that live on decaying plants and animals are important. These are recyclers, which means they help change dead things into chemicals which plants need to grow, so that the plants may use them over and over again. Others are pollinators, as they carry pollen from flower to flower. Many kinds of animals and birds feed on flies.

Flight

All flies use only one pair of wings to fly with. Their back wings, which are very small, are used only to balance them as they fly. The movement of the wings is very fast in many flies. Houseflies beat their wings about 200 times each second, mosquitoes about 600 times and some of the smallest midges at a rate of over 1,000 times a second.

Shapes

Flies vary a lot in shape. One big group, that includes all the mosquitoes and midges, have slender, soft bodies. The daddy-long-legs, which is easy to see because it is so large, also belongs to this group. It is harmless, but many of the adults in this group have biting and sucking mouthparts and the females feed on the blood of mammals or birds.

A second group, which includes the horseflies and clegs, have short, hard bodies. The females also feed on blood, although the males feed only on plant juices. The third and largest group of the flies is the one which includes the houseflies and hoverflies. All of these have short, well armoured bodies, and most feed on liquids of various kinds. A very small number of these flies feed on blood.

Grubs

Flies spend the first part of their lives as larvae, also called grubs or maggots. The larvae live in many different ways. The blind maggots which live in the flesh of dead mammals or birds are the most familiar. Other kinds live in the soil, hunting small animals. Others live in water. One of the strangest of these is the rat-tailed maggot of one of the hoverflies. This can survive in polluted water, for it pushes a long tube, like a snorkel, up to the surface to breathe. Some larvae are harmful to cattle and other animals, as the adults lay their eggs on the skin and the larvae burrow in to become parasites.

Mosquitoes

Female mosquitoes feed on blood, which gives them the protein they need to lay their eggs. The males eat nothing but nectar, or sugary juices from plants. When a female mosquito feeds, she uses her piercing tube-like mouthparts to cut through the skin of her victim, usually a mammal or bird. Then she probes about to find a tiny blood vessel. Before she begins to suck up the blood, she injects a tiny amount of saliva, which contains a substance to stop the blood clotting. The mosquito's drinking tube is so fine that the blood would certainly harden and block it if she did not do so. Anybody who has been

bitten by a mosquito knows that the bite usually comes up in a bump. This is because the saliva contains a chemical which irritates the skin. If the mosquito has bitten somebody whose blood contains malaria germs, or those of some other diseases, such as yellow fever, the germs will get into her salivary glands and she will infect the next person she bites.

Dragonflies

Dragonflies swoop and speed over streams and ponds. They are the fastest flying of all insects, and some may reach a speed of 57 km/h (35 mph). Dragonflies are not true flies because they have four wings. They are very agile in flight, and they can even fly backwards. Dragonflies are hunters, catching and eating other insects.

When you see dragonflies by water, you may notice that they fly up and down the bank. This is because the males defend a territory. If a female comes along, the male grabs her by the back of the neck. They mate on the wing and afterwards often stay together while the female lays her eggs.

The nymphs (larvae) that hatch from the eggs live and grow in the water, feeding on all sorts of small creatures, up to the size of tadpoles. Food is caught by the mask, a sort of hooked arm which the nymph shoots out from its face. This nymph stage may last two or three years.

Mosquitoes lay their eggs in ponds, ditches, puddles, flooded tyre tracks or even discarded cans. In warm climates females lay over 1,000 eggs at a time; in cooler regions between 100 and 300.

A dragonfly's eyes take up most of the space on its head, for these insects have very good sight. They can see food up to 40 m away. Their sense of smell is poor, and their antennae are tiny and threadlike.

◀ **Red heather dragonfly. The dragonfly can use its six legs for perching but not for walking.**

Bees

▶ Bumble-bee visiting flower. Her pollen baskets can be seen clearly.

Most people have seen honey-bees searching flowers for nectar and pollen. Honey-bees, and their close relatives, the bumble-bees, like ants and termites, live in family groups. Each hive or nest is the home of a large number of bees and their mother, the queen bee. The grubs that hatch from the eggs she lays are tended by worker bees. These are females whose sex organs are not developed and so they cannot lay eggs. A small number of the bees in a hive are males, or drones. These do not help to make stores of pollen and honey, or look after the grubs. Their job is to mate with young queen bees. After this the drones die. The queens survive to be mothers of new huge families in other nests.

Worker bees also have short lives, dying at about six weeks. Some workers survive the winter, and these live for several months. The queen bee can survive for up to five years, so the honey-bees' nest is quite long-lived. Bumble-bee queens do not live so long, dying, with the rest of their family, at the end of the summer. Only the young bumble-bee queens, which have mated, survive the winter. It is a sure sign of spring when you see the new queen bumble-bees looking for suitable spots for their nests.

Honey

Bees make honey from nectar, which they suck from flowers. They can do this because their jaws form a tube, like a built-in drinking straw. As a bee searches for nectar, pollen from the flowers gets stuck on her hairy coat. She combs this off and presses it into her 'pollen baskets' which are on her hind legs. The pollen is used to feed the grubs for most of their lives.

As well as honey-bees and bumble-bees, there are many species of 'solitary' bees. In these species, the females lay their eggs in tiny nests which they stock with food. They die before the grubs hatch.

BEE DANCE

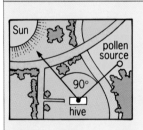

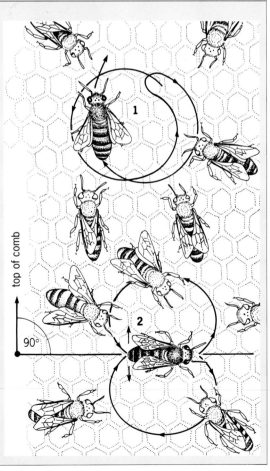

A worker bee who has found food is able to communicate the direction and distance of the food to her companions by a 'waggle dance'. If the food is nearby she performs a simple round dance; if a long way off a figure of eight dance is performed. The number of waggles in the dance tells the workers how far away the food is. The direction the bee is moving as she waggles, shows the direction of the food in relation to the sun.

WORKER BEES

Worker bees change their jobs as they get older. They clean empty cells in the honeycomb ready for eggs from the queen or honey and pollen from older workers.

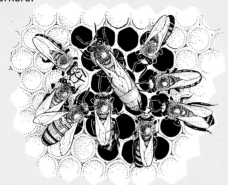

They feed young developing bees (larvae), and then start producing wax to repair and make new honeycomb.

They become guards which kill or drive away wasps, mice and other honey thieves, or beat their wings to drive fresh air into the hive.

Finally they visit flowers to collect nectar and pollen.

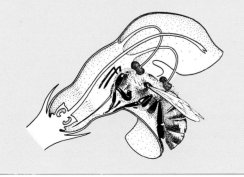

Wasps

Wasps are insects with yellow and black stripes. These bright colours act as a warning that the wasp can protect itself with a sting.

Many wasps live in family groups which are all the offspring of one female, called the queen. These are called social wasps. Their nests are formed of a kind of paper.

◄ These large wasps are called paper wasps. The sterile female workers continue to enlarge the nest that their mother the queen wasp began. The queen wasp will lay an egg in each hexagonal cell.

The wasps make this by chewing up dead wood and mixing it with their saliva. The cells of the wasp's nest are hexagonal and the nest is formed in a series of floors, connected to each other by paper pillars. The grubs living in the nest are fed on the flesh of other animals, particularly insects. Early in the summer, when many grubs are being reared, wasps are very useful animals, as they kill many pests for food. The adults themselves need sugars for energy and feed only on nectar, fruit and tree sap. Most adults are sterile female workers but by late summer fully sexed males and females have been produced. These breed, and then the whole colony, which might number 50,000 wasps, dies with the arrival of cold weather. Only the young mated queens survive in hibernation, to emerge next spring.

As well as the social wasps, there are many species which do not live in family groups and lay their eggs in individual nests.

Distribution
Worldwide

Largest
Mason bee, up to 3·8 cm long

Smallest
Fairy fly (a parasite wasp) less than 1 mm

Ants

▶Leaf cutter ants slice off parts of leaves and carry them back to their nests. They chew the leaves into a pulp and use them as fertilizer for fungus. The ants cultivate the fungus in 'gardens', to eat.

Distribution
Worldwide

Largest ant
Bulldog ant, 2·5 cm long

Smallest ant
Some Argentine ants are less than 2 mm

Ants are insects which always live in groups or colonies. There may be 100,000 ants in a colony but they all have the same mother. She is called the queen ant. The ants that you are most likely to see are called workers. These are all females, yet they are unable to lay eggs, for their sex organs are not fully developed.

Most ants do not have wings, as they live

▶ Red ant worker collecting honeydew from aphids on a nettle stem. The ant will actually carry the aphids to suitable plants.

in sheltered nests, where wings would get in the way. But for a short time each year, usually on a warm, muggy day, the air is full of flying ants. These are the males and the egg-laying females, leaving the nest for their mating flight. After mating, the males die, but the females begin to make new nests to lay eggs in. Their wings break off and the muscles which enabled them to fly are used to give them energy until the first young workers hatch. From then on the workers collect food for themselves, their young sisters and the queen. Some of the later workers may become soldiers, growing large and helping to protect the nest, by biting and squirting acid at enemies.

Ants feed on many kinds of food. Some hunt other animals, some feed on seeds and some eat a kind of fungus that they grow on a compost of leaves especially gathered. Most ants like sweet things and some 'milk' aphids of their honeydew. In most of the things that ants do their behaviour is innate, which means they do not have to think about it, or learn how to do it.

Termites

Termites live only in the warmer parts of the world. Like ants and bees they are social insects. Some kinds make very large nests, which may be 7 m (23 ft) in height and house over 1 million insects. Termite mounds can be immensely strong. When they are built on ground needed for cultivation, sometimes even bulldozers cannot flatten them and explosives are needed to level them.

At a certain time each year, numbers of winged termites emerge. After a brief flight they lose their wings and each male pairs with a female. The termite nest includes a queen, who is the mother of all of the insects in the nest, and a king, who is their father. The queen's body, swollen with eggs, may measure 10 cm (4 in) in length. She cannot move, but all her needs are attended to by her worker children.

Unlike bees and ants the young termites hatch out as small replicas of their parents; there are no larval and pupal stages. They eat only plant materials and because of their numbers they may be pests, damaging crops or the timbers of buildings. The termite is the longest lived insect. The queen usually lives for 15-20 years, but there are records of termites living up to 50 years.

Those termites not involved with reproduction are either workers or soldiers. Workers search for food outside the nest. When they have brought it back they must feed all the other termites. The soldiers, like the king and queen, are unable to feed without help. The soldiers protect the nest from ants and other invaders.

▼ Termite mound in West Africa. This mound was constructed by termite workers from soil mixed with saliva. Inside there are many tunnels and chambers connecting together.

▼ African termite workers repairing damage to earth channels running up inside a dead tree trunk which is part of their nest. Most termites are workers. They are blind and wingless with soft pale bodies. Only their heads and feet are covered with a hard protective material.

Spiders and scorpions

► **Female red-kneed tarantula. Some tarantulas are poisonous, but less dangerous than most people think.**

Spiders, like insects, have jointed legs and bodies which are made in sections or segments. But, unlike an insect, a spider's body consists of two, not three parts, and it has eight, not six legs. Also spiders cannot fly, although baby spiders and small adult types may 'parachute' on long silk threads.

All spiders can make silk. It is pushed from special organs called spinnerets which are at the back of the body. Silk is formed as a liquid but hardens instantly on contact with air. Spiders use silk to protect their eggs and to wrap up prey. Some use it to make traps called webs to catch their prey in.

All spiders are carnivores. They feed mainly on the flesh of insects or other tiny creatures, although the largest species may catch animals as big as small birds and mice. When a spider has caught its prey, it uses pointed fangs to inject venom (poison). This paralyses the prey and also contains digestive juices which break down the prey's flesh, making it liquid. The spider then feeds by sucking up this liquid meal.

Some spiders make sticky, circular orb webs, but there are other sorts of trap, including hammock webs, funnel webs and trap-door traps. When an insect blunders into a web, the spider rushes out before it can escape, wraps its victim in silk and then injects it with venom.

Not all spiders build webs. Wolf spiders have larger eyes than web-building types and rely entirely on speed and strength to outrun and overcome their prey.

Most spiders have very small eyes and are very short-sighted but jumping spiders have two huge eyes which look forwards and smaller ones looking sideways and backwards. They move like a cat stalking a bird until in jumping range of a fly. Then

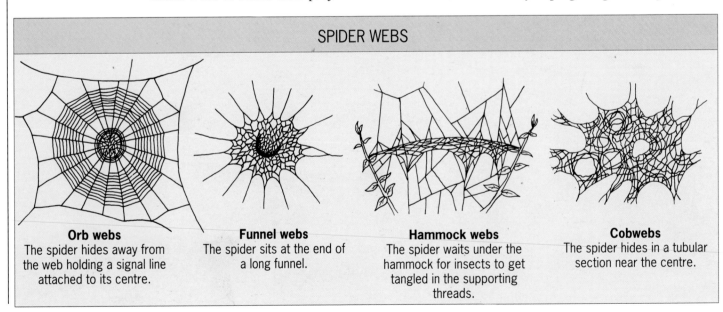

SPIDER WEBS

Orb webs
The spider hides away from the web holding a signal line attached to its centre.

Funnel webs
The spider sits at the end of a long funnel.

Hammock webs
The spider waits under the hammock for insects to get tangled in the supporting threads.

Cobwebs
The spider hides in a tubular section near the centre.

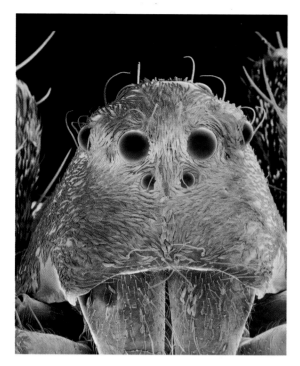

quickly out of the water and back again to trap a layer of air under their thick coat of hairs. A water spider's web is dome-shaped and full of air shaken from its body. It lives here while waiting for tiny water creatures to swim by.

◀ The head of a green lynx spider magnified 13 times. It has eight eyes which give it excellent vision.

Scorpions

Scorpions live mainly in the warmer parts of the world. They are rarely seen, as they are solitary animals which hide during the daytime and come out at night to hunt.

They feed chiefly on insects and other small creatures, which they kill using their large claws to tear them apart. If the prey resists, the scorpion uses the poisonous sting at the end of its tail. The sting is also used in defence against larger enemies such as monkeys. Their poison can be dangerous to human beings as well.

During the breeding season scorpions have an elaborate pattern of courtship before mating. This looks like a dance as the male guides the female over his sperm.

Young scorpions are born alive, one or two at a time, over several weeks. The baby scorpions ride on their mother's back for protection, until they moult their skin for the first time.

Distribution
Virtually worldwide (scorpions in warmer parts only)

Largest spider
More than 10 cm long (the leg span may be twice this)

Largest scorpion
About 18 cm long

Smallest spider
Less than 1 mm long

Smallest scorpion
About 1 cm long

Lifespan
Some large spiders have survived for 15 years in captivity. Most probably live for much less than this.

Biggest webs
Some webs spun by orb-weaver spiders have measured 5·7 m around the edge.

they leap onto the insect's back and bite it with their fangs.

Spitting spiders get their name from their method of catching insects. They spit a stream of poisonous glue at them. This sticks the insect firmly to the ground so that the spider can eat it at leisure.

A few spiders live entirely under water and even build an underwater web. They swim to the surface regularly and lift themselves

◀ A female scorpion carrying her young on her back for safety. This scorpion is in Florida.

Centipedes and millipedes

► The centipede's flattened body enables it to squeeze through narrow spaces in the soil or rotten wood. Its eyesight is poor, but its long antennae help it to track its prey. This is killed by poison from fangs formed from the first pair of legs.

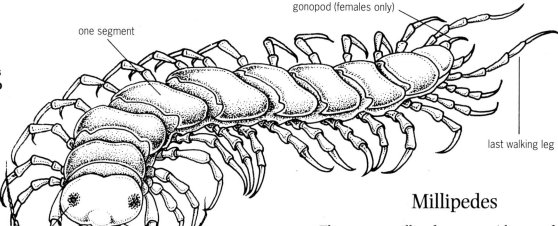

Distribution
Worldwide

Largest
A centipede over 30 cm in length. This species sometimes eats mice and lizards as well as insects.

Smallest
A millipede about 2 mm long

The name centipede means 'hundred feet' though most centipedes have fewer than this. Many have as few as fifteen pairs of legs. Some have even less than this when they first hatch, but as they grow longer they develop more legs. Centipedes have been known to have up to 177 pairs of legs.

Centipedes' bodies are made up of a number of similar parts, called segments. Most of these have a single pair of legs. Centipedes have rather flat bodies, which enable them to squeeze through narrow spaces. They move fast, for they are hunters, tracking insects, grubs and worms which are their main food. They use poison fangs to overcome their prey.

Some tropical centipedes can give an unpleasant bite if they are handled, but most are entirely harmless to humans.

►Millipedes have a row of stink glands along their sides from which they produce unpleasant chemicals when disturbed. Some protect themselves by rolling up into a tight ball. Most millipedes are dull-coloured, but a few tropical kinds are brightly coloured. This is an additional warning to predators.

Millipedes

The name millipede means 'thousand feet'. This is an exaggeration, as no millipede has more than 400 feet. Even so, this is more than any other animal. Millipedes are slow-moving, but their legs provide enough power to burrow through leaf litter and loose soil to search for soft or decaying plants to eat. Those in forests are important recyclers, returning chemicals to the soil for plants to use again. In gardens they are considered pests.

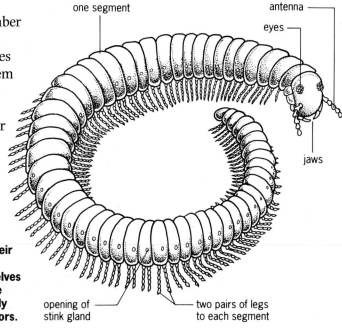

Worms

Very many kinds of long, thin animals without backbones are called 'worms', but the word is most often used for earthworms.

An earthworm has a head and a tail end, but most of its body is made up of segments which are very similar to each other. Each of these segments has a small number of stiff hairs on it. These grip the sides of the worm's tunnel so it is very difficult to pull the worm out.

Some earthworms eat the soil as they burrow, and digest tiny scraps of plant and animal material that they get from it. Other kinds feed on leaves that they pull down into their burrows.

There are huge numbers of earth-worms in the soil. An area the size of a football pitch could be the home to half a tonne of earthworms, and in very rich farmland there could be 24 times as many.

Worms' burrows allow air and rain to reach the roots of plants. Their droppings,

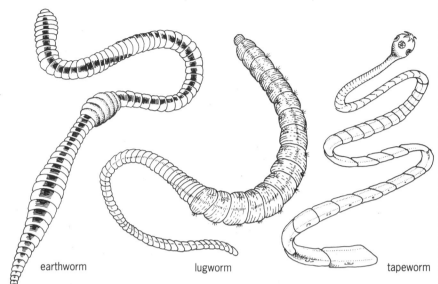

earthworm   lugworm   tapeworm

which are the wormcasts you can see on the surface of the ground, contain minerals which fertilize the soil. As well as this, worms are important as the chief food of many animals, including birds, moles and badgers. Some tropical relatives of the earthworms can grow into two new worms if the animal is cut in two. In the cooler parts of the world a worm may be able to regrow one part of itself, but not both.

▲ The earthworm with its marine relative the lugworm and a tapeworm, which is unrelated.

Distribution
Everywhere except where the soil is frozen, or too dry

Largest earthworm
The giant Australian earthworm, over 3 m long

Smallest worm
A water worm, about 6 mm long

◄ A member of one of the 80 families of ragworm. All ragworms are sea animals. Some live in deep oceans, others burrow in the seashore.

Slugs and snails

▲ The large Roman snail with a cluster of eggs. Roman snails are eaten by many other animals including humans.

To most people, slugs and snails are slow, slimy pests. While it is true that neither slugs nor snails can move very fast, only a few kinds are serious pests.

The great difference between snails and slugs is that in times of danger the snail can pull its soft body into a single usually coiled shell. Sea snails usually have heavy shells, as the shell is supported by the water. An exception is the sea butterflies, which live in the surface waters of the oceans and have shells as fragile as fine glass. Slugs may have a small shell, or an internal shell, but never one in which they can take refuge.

In most other ways snails and slugs are very similar. Both glide along on a large, muscular foot. Slugs and land snails ease their way with slime, which you can see after the animal has passed. Both snails and slugs have simple eyes, which are sometimes on tentacles. They may also have other tentacles which help them to feel and smell. Both slugs and snails have a mouth on the underside of the head. This contains very many tiny teeth. A garden snail may have about 14,000 teeth in its mouth. They are arranged in rows on a ribbon-like tongue, which is called a radula. This works like a file, to rasp away at food.

Most slugs and snails are hermaphrodites, which means individuals have both male and female sex organs. But they still need to mate to reproduce, as they do not fertilize themselves.

Snails

Snails are found almost everywhere: there are snails in rivers, lakes and in the sea, as well as on land. Land snails, like slugs, need damp conditions. When it is dry they seal themselves into their shells with a layer of slime, and remain inactive until it rains.

Most land snails feed on rotting plants. It is only in tidy gardens where decaying matter has been removed that they feed on seedlings and fresh leaves. Water snails feed on water plants and sometimes dead animals. Some snails feed on other animals and have fewer, but stronger teeth on their radulae. On the seashore you may sometimes find a mussel or other bivalve shell with a neat hole bored in it. This is the work of the necklace shell or one of its relatives, which rasps through the armour of the bivalve to get at the helpless animal inside. The cone shells, which are tropical sea snails, even feed on fish. These are stilled with a nerve poison injected by a single, hypodermic-like tooth at the end of the radula.

Slugs

Slugs look like snails without their shells. Many slugs do actually have shells, however, but they are so small as to be difficult to see, or are actually hidden within the slug's body.

Most slugs feed on a variety of foodstuffs including vegetation, both rotting and fresh, fungi, tubers and carrion. Shelled slugs also feed on earthworms which they swallow whole. They find their food by smell, using their tentacles.

◄ Like snails, slugs are also hermaphrodites (have both male and female sex organs). These mating slugs are exchanging sperm; later both will lay eggs. The breathing hole can be seen clearly on one slug.

Sea slugs

The sea slugs are some of the most brightly coloured of all animals. In some sea slugs the bright colours warn predators that they taste nasty, but some of the most colourful live in the deep sea where there is not enough light to see them. The many flaps of skin act a little like gills, providing a large surface area to absorb oxygen from the surrounding water. Though these are soft-bodied, they are far from helpless. Most feed on jellyfish and sea anemones. They are immune to the stings of such creatures, and are even able to transfer these stings after swallowing them, to their own skins for protection, though nobody is sure how they do this.

Distribution
Most live in the sea, but some live in fresh water and some on land, even in deserts.

Largest sea snail
The baler shell, from the Australian Barrier Reef, 60 cm long

Largest land snail
Giant land snail, *Achatina fulica*, originally from Africa, now found in many parts of the tropics, up to 30 cm long

◄ A sea slug makes its way across part of the Great Barrier Reef, Australia. You are looking down at the top of the slug.

Shellfish

▶ Around the edge of this scallop's shell is a fringe of tentacles sensitive to touch, and a row of eyes.

Distribution
Common in the sea, but a few snails and bivalves live in fresh water. Many snails and slugs live on dry land.

Heaviest mollusc with a shell
Giant clam may weigh up to 454 kg

Monoplacophora
Neopilina

Polyplacophora
chiton

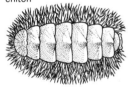

Gastropoda
snail

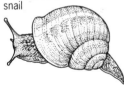

Scaphopoda
tusk shell

Bivalvia
scallop

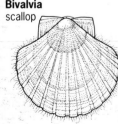

Many molluscs have thick, heavy shells. Inside the shell there is a soft body which usually includes a head, a muscular foot, and breathing, digestive and sex organs. These are covered with a flap of skin called the mantle which manufactures the shell. Molluscs with shells are called shellfish, and are divided into different groups.

Monoplacophora (8 species). Found in deep water off the coast of North and South America. They could be called living fossils, for their ancestors lived over 500 million years ago. They look like limpets and have several sets of gills.

Polyplacophora (550 species). These are the chitons, living on the seashore or in shallow water. They have a shell made of eight plates, and a strong foot which clamps them onto rocks firmly enough to withstand the battering waves. They have no tentacles or eyes, and feed by scraping tiny plants and animals from rocks with their tongues.

Gastropoda (35,000 species). Including snails, limpets, whelks, and land and sea slugs. They have a head with tentacles and eyes and move on a muscular foot. Most have a single shell, which in snails is coiled. They live in many different places including deserts, oceans and fresh water. They feed on both plants and animals.

Scaphopoda (350 species). These are called tusk shells as they look like tiny elephant tusks. They live deep under the sand out of reach of the tides, trapping food using tentacles armed with suckers.

Bivalvia (8,000 species). They have a hinged shell made up of two pieces. All live in water, and many can burrow in sand or mud using their foot. Water is sucked inside the shells, where the gills remove the oxygen and tiny fragments of food.

Crustaceans

Crustaceans, such as lobsters, crabs and shrimps, are also sometimes known as shellfish because of their hard, shell-like skeletons on the outsides of their bodies.

Octopuses and squids

Octopuses

Octopuses are related to snails. They do not have the protection of a shell, but their bodies are flexible, so they can squeeze into small holes where they are safe from enemies such as conger eels.

The main part of an octopus's body is a bag of skin and muscle. Inside this are the gills and other soft parts. At the front end, the head is attached to one side of the bag. When the mouth of the bag is open, water flows in to give oxygen to the gills. The bag can then be tightened round the neck and the water forced out through a tube. The jet of water is quite strong, so the octopus is jet-propelled and can move very quickly indeed.

Octopuses can see well, for they have large eyes, very much like the eyes of mammals in their structure. They are all hunters, feeding on creatures such as crabs, which they catch and hold with suckers on the eight long arms surrounding the mouth. When an octopus catches its prey, a bite from its horny beak injects a nerve poison so that even a strong animal is quickly overcome. Octopuses are mostly quite harmless to humans.

Squids

Squids are also relatives of the snail, but they have no shells. Instead they have a stiff, horny support inside their bag-like bodies. This is called the pen. As squids also have ink sacs, they are sometimes called the pen and ink animals. The head, with its large eyes and big brain, is attached at the front of the body bag. Eight long arms surround the mouth, and there are also two even longer tentacles.

Squids live mostly in the open ocean. They propel themselves with jets of water. Some move so quickly that they can become airborne and skim over the waves for a distance of 20 m (60 ft) or more. Squids feed mainly on fish, which they catch with their long tentacles. Like the arms, these carry suckers, which often have claws to help hold the slippery prey. Squids are themselves the food for many kinds of animals. Giant squids which live in the deep sea are an important part of the food of sperm whales.

In the darkness of the deep sea, squids often use brightly coloured light organs to signal to each other and dazzle attackers. Usually there is at least one light organ near to the eyes, so that the squid will not be blinded by the light which may be produced by a hunting fish

Distribution
In all the oceans of the world

Largest octopus
Pacific octopus, armspan about 7 m (body only about 0·5 m in length)

Smallest octopus
Several species have armspans of only about 5 cm.

Largest squid
Giant squids up to 20 m

Smallest squid
Sandalops pathopis, a deep sea squid, measuring about 2·5 cm.

◄ An octopus searches for food on the ocean bottom.

▼ Cuttlefish are closely related to squid and octopus. When alarmed they release a cloud of ink-like pigment, change colour, and shoot away by jet propulsion.

Crabs and lobsters

Distribution
On the edges of the seas of the world. A few crabs live in deep water and some live on land. Lobsters are also found in many rivers outside the tropics

Largest lobster
Northern lobster *Homarus americanus*. Body over 50 cm long. The crushing claw may be as big as a man's head. Greatest weight recorded 20·2 kg.

Largest crab
Japanese spider crab, leg-span measures over 2·6 m

Smallest species
Includes the pea crabs, which are about the size of a pea when adult

The word 'crustacea' means 'crusty ones'. This is a suitable name for a group of animals which all have a jointed crust or shell to support and protect them. Sometimes this is very thick, as the horny material (chitin) from which it is made may be strengthened with a substance like chalk. Crabs and lobsters, for instance, are very effectively armoured in this way.

Almost all crustaceans live in water. Those which live on land, like woodlice, are not as well waterproofed as their distant relatives the insects and spiders, so they can exist only in damp places, where they are in no danger of drying out.

Crabs

The crab has a body which is wider than it is long. The head and the middle part are joined together to form a single, heavily armoured unit. The abdomen is small, and tucked up below the main part of the body. All crabs have ten legs, the front pair of which usually end in large claws. The crab uses these to defend itself and to tear up its food. One claw maybe bigger than the other, in male fiddler crabs for example, one claw is very much larger. Crabs usually

walk sideways, as they can move more quickly this way. Some crabs, such as the ghost crabs of the tropics, are particularly fast.

Most crabs spend all of their lives in the sea, although some, like the shore crab, can stand short periods out of the water at low tide. The few kinds that live in fresh water have to return to the sea to breed. Hermit crabs spend a lot of time out of water. These are not true crabs as, like lobsters they have long abdomens. Their abdomens are soft, without the layer of protective armour that covers the front of their bodies. They protect themselves by tucking their soft abdomens into the shells of dead sea snails.

▼ **The common shore crab lives in estuaries as well as in the sea, in Europe.**

Lobsters

Lobsters are giants among crustaceans and they are also the longest-lived. Some may live for up to 100 years or more. Normally lobsters eat dead animals, but will sometimes eat live ones and occasionally each other. They use their huge claws to crush and tear their food. Lobsters spend most of their time in rock crevices, coming out only to feed. They test their surroundings with their long antennae, ready to protect themselves with their claws. If need be they can swim, or shoot backwards through the water at great speed.

Freshwater lobsters are called crayfish, and are very much like their sea-living relatives. They are widespread in lakes and rivers. The spiny lobsters or crawfish are lobster-like sea crustaceans which do not have claws, but defend themselves with long, spiny, whip-like antennae.

Prawns

Prawns and shrimps are small relatives of the crabs and lobsters. Unlike their heavyweight cousins, they have only a light exoskeleton (shell). They may have small pincers on their first pair of legs, but no powerful crushing or tearing claws. Snapping prawns, however, do have one well developed pincer, which they can snap to make a very loud noise. The noise is so loud it can stun the prawns' prey, and also deter enemies.

Generally the bodies of prawns are rather flattened from side to side. This helps to make them streamlined for swimming. Most prawns and shrimps live in shallow seas. They have stalked eyes, and two pairs of delicate feelers for exploring scent and shape. Almost all of them are scavengers, eating the remains of dead sea creatures.

▲ An Atlantic prawn. This is a deep sea species and, like many crustaceans of the dark depths of the oceans, is red in colour.

◄ Pacific lobster. The tiny bristles covering the lobster's body are sense organs sensitive to touch and chemicals in the water. The lobster's antennae are balancing organs as well as sense organs, helping the lobster to tell which way up in the water it is.

WOODLICE

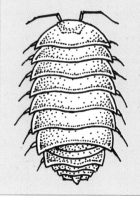

Woodlice have armoured bodies and seven pairs of walking legs. They are crustaceans, not insects. Woodlice live in damp places, because they breathe through gills which can only work if they are moist.

Woodlice feed mainly on rotting plants. They protect themselves from enemies, such as spiders and centipedes, by producing a sticky fluid or rolling themselves into a tight ball. Female woodlice lay up to 200 eggs, which they carry with them. The baby woodlice also often stay with their mother for some weeks after hatching. They take about two years to become fully mature.

Coral

▶Coral reef in the New Hebrides.

The Great Barrier Reef, off the east coast of Australia, is so large that it can be seen from the Moon. It is over 2,000 km (1,250 miles) long.

Largest solitary coral
Mushroom coral, about 30 cm long

Distribution
Reef-building corals found in warm, shallow, tropical seas.
Solitary corals found also in dark, cold, deep ocean waters.

Corals are small animals related to sea anemones. Each coral animal is called a polyp. Their bodies are filled with fluid and are plastic in shape. The mouth end is ringed with stinging tentacles which are used to catch passing water creatures. The polyp produces a hard limestone skeleton around itself in the shape of a cup. Even after the polyp has died, the hard skeleton remains. Corals often look dead because most polyps only stretch out their tentacles to feed at night. By day they shrink into their cups for protection.

From time to time, the polyps release sperm and eggs into the water. The fertilized eggs hatch into tiny swimming larvae. Some of these may drift on the ocean currents, and help to disperse the corals around the ocean. Many coral polyps are solitary, but some live together in colonies.

Coral reefs

Some coral polyps are formed as buds on existing polyps. These new polyps grow but do not separate completely from their parents and so a colony is built up. Coral reefs are made up of the skeletons of millions of polyps.

Reef-building corals can grow only in clear, clean water no deeper than 50 m (160 ft), and no colder than 18°C (65°F). Since the last ice age, the sea-level has been rising, so the reefs have been growing up towards the light. Some coral reefs are thousands of feet thick.

Coral reefs are home to many different animals. Sea slugs, starfish, sea urchins and many fish feed on the corals. Other animals, such as crabs and shrimps, live in the crevices in the reef. Other fish, squid and octopus come to feed on them. Sponges, sea squirts and barnacles grow amongst the corals. They filter food from the water. Worms wriggle among the corals, and moray eels and lobsters hide in the coral caves. Larger predators such as reef sharks and barracudas are attracted to the reef from the ocean.

SEA ANEMONES

Sea anemones live attached to rocks and breakwaters on the sea-shore and in shallow water. They are closely related to coral but are entirely soft-bodied.

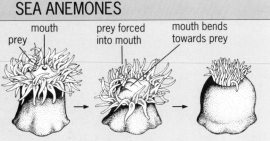

mouth
prey
prey forced into mouth
mouth bends towards prey

Jellyfish

◀ **The sea nettle as its name implies, will sting if touched.**

Distribution
In all the oceans of the world, often in shallow water. A very few kinds live in fresh water.

Largest true jellyfish
Cyanea arctica, over 2 m across the bell; the tentacles trail over 65 m.

Most poisonous jellyfish
The sea wasps, which live in warm water near to the coast of Australia, have caused the death of a number of humans.

Jellyfish are not true fish, but their name is a suitable one, because they swim or float in the water and much of their bell-shaped bodies is made up of a stiff, jelly-like material. From the edge of the bell, long tentacles trail into the sea, while the mouthparts hang from its centre. Jellyfish are sometimes called 'medusas', after the creature in Greek myth which could turn living things to stone. Jellyfish cannot do this, but any animal which touches the tentacles finds that these are covered with powerful stinging cells, much like those on the tentacles of sea anemones. The sting cells are strong enough to paralyse active prey, usually fish, shrimps or other aquatic animals on which most jellyfish feed.

Several related, but different sorts of creatures are often referred to as jellyfish. These include the Portuguese man-of-war. Jellyfish are closely related to sea anemones.

Portuguese man-of-war

The Portuguese man-of-war may look like a jellyfish, but it is actually a colony of polyps (small coral-like animals) living together. Some of the polyps look like tentacles and sting to protect the colony; others take in food and some are specialized for reproduction.

▶ **A sting cell contains a coiled, hollow tube with sharp hooks near the end. When a fish or other prey touches the trigger, the tube shoots out like a harpoon. Its hooks drill a hole in the prey's skin through which poison is squirted.**

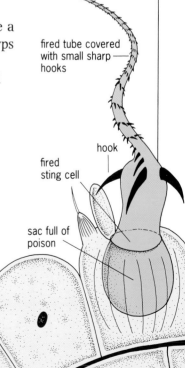

fired tube covered with small sharp hooks

hook

fired sting cell

sac full of poison

unfired sting cell

trigger

The human body

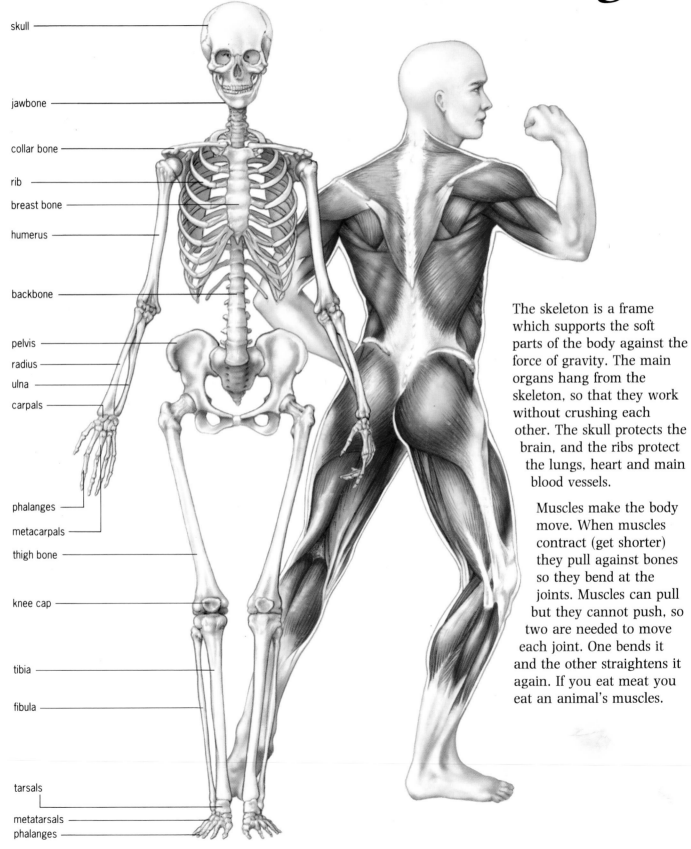

skull

jawbone

collar bone

rib

breast bone

humerus

backbone

pelvis

radius

ulna

carpals

phalanges

metacarpals

thigh bone

knee cap

tibia

fibula

tarsals

metatarsals

phalanges

The skeleton is a frame which supports the soft parts of the body against the force of gravity. The main organs hang from the skeleton, so that they work without crushing each other. The skull protects the brain, and the ribs protect the lungs, heart and main blood vessels.

Muscles make the body move. When muscles contract (get shorter) they pull against bones so they bend at the joints. Muscles can pull but they cannot push, so two are needed to move each joint. One bends it and the other straightens it again. If you eat meat you eat an animal's muscles.

Bones

Bones are alive. This is why they can mend and regrow after they break. They are as strong as some kinds of steel, but only one-fifth as heavy. So they form a firm, light skeleton on which are attached the soft parts of the body. Bones are made from a mixture of the tough protein collagen, and hard mineral crystals containing calcium and phosphorus. This mixture gives the bones their strength.

At the centre of many bones is a soft tissue called bone marrow. This contains blood vessels that supply the bone with food and oxygen. The marrow is also the place where new red and white blood cells are continually made. Embedded in the hard part of bone are the cells that make the actual bone material.

As a baby grows in its mother's womb, its bones slowly develop. To begin with they are made of the softer, gristly substance called cartilage. During growth the cartilage is mainly turned into bone, apart from those parts that remain bendy like the tip of the nose and the ears. Cartilage is still found in an adult's bones. It forms the smooth surfaces where bones slide against one another at joints.

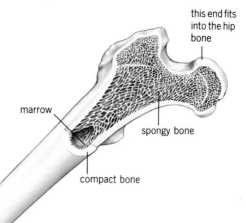

this end fits into the hip bone

marrow

spongy bone

compact bone

shaft

this end forms part of knee joint

◀ The thigh bone is the longest bone in the body. Its head fits into a socket in the hip bone, and the opposite end forms part of the knee joint.

Muscles

Almost all animals have muscles. Muscles work by contracting (getting shorter). They cannot lengthen themselves, but they can be stretched by other muscles pulling at them. Muscles contract when they receive nerve impulses (messages) from the nervous system. They need a lot of energy, supplied by food. In people there are three types of muscles. The first type is attached to the bones and is used to move the body. This is called voluntary muscle because it only works when you want it to. When you want to move, it pulls against your skeleton, bending it at the joints. The second type is called involuntary muscle because it can contract without you thinking about it. An example is muscles around the gut which push food along it. The third type is found in the heart. This is the cardiac muscle. It can work continuously for years without getting tired.

Animal bones are constructed in the same way as human bones.

You have 639 muscles of the type that move your body. These make up almost half of your total weight.
You sit on the largest and strongest muscles in your body. These are the muscles around your bottom, which you use to rise from a sitting position, or climb a hill.

BROKEN BONES

If you break a bone it is called a fracture. A bone should be set back in its proper position as soon as possible. A plaster cast may be needed to keep it in place. An X-ray will show how badly the bone is broken.

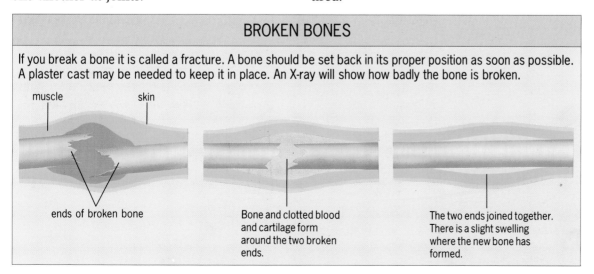

muscle

skin

ends of broken bone

Bone and clotted blood and cartilage form around the two broken ends.

The two ends joined together. There is a slight swelling where the new bone has formed.

The heart

vein from upper body

aorta

artery to left lung

veins from left lung

left atrium

left ventricle

right atrium

coronary artery

right ventricle

vein from lower body

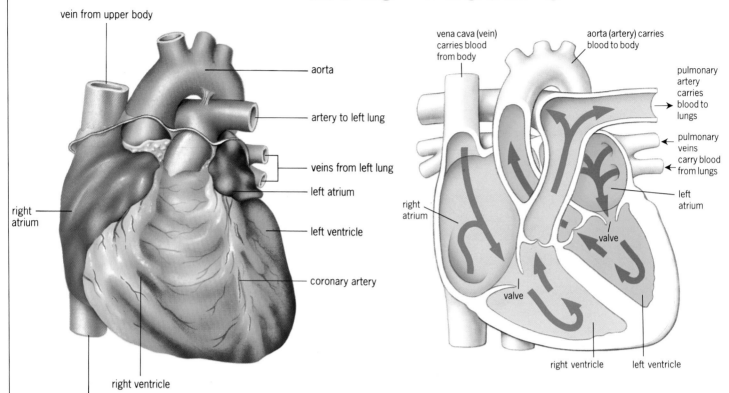

vena cava (vein) carries blood from body

aorta (artery) carries blood to body

pulmonary artery carries blood to lungs

pulmonary veins carry blood from lungs

right atrium

left atrium

valve

valve

right ventricle   left ventricle

▲ The heart seen from the front. The coronary artery supplies the heart's muscle with food.

The cross section shows what the heart would look like sliced open. The atria and ventricles are hollow with muscular walls. Valves between the atria and ventricles and between the atria and arteries ensure that the blood flow is only one way.

A heart is a pump made of muscle, which pumps blood around the body. The blood is pumped through tubes called blood vessels or in spaces called sinuses. Hearts like this are found in all backboned animals and in many of the larger types of animals without backbones. Earthworms, crabs, insects, snails and squids all have hearts that pump their blood.

In humans, the heart is a large organ in the middle of the chest. It is made of four muscular chambers: two atria and two ventricles. Their strong contractions are the heartbeats we feel in our chests.

Blood pushed out from the heart passes along thick-walled blood vessels called arteries. These come close to the skin surface at the wrist and in the neck, and you can feel your pulse. This is the wave of blood being pushed by a heartbeat along the artery. So measuring your pulse rate tells you how fast your heart is beating. A normal rate is between 65 and 85 beats per minute for an adult, and about 90 beats a minute for a seven-year-old.

HEART BEATS

Between beats the heart relaxes and fills with blood from the veins. Valves prevent blood entering through the arteries.

Atria contract and blood is forced from them into the ventricles.

Ventricles contract and blood is forced into the arteries. Valves prevent blood flowing back into the atria. The atria start to fill with blood again.

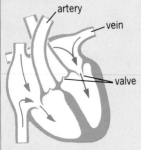

artery

vein

valve

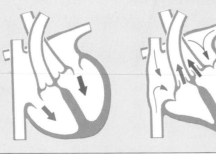

How blood circulates

The movement of the blood around the body is called circulation. Blood passes out of the heart to the body or the lungs along arteries. It then goes through very thin blood vessels called capillaries. These then join up into thin-walled veins, which take the blood back to the heart to be circulated again. The left side of the heart takes blood from the lungs and pushes it round the body. The right side gets it back from the body and pushes it to the lungs.

The beating rate of the heart is under the control of the brain. If your body needs to work hard, because you are running, your brain instructs your heart to speed up. This means the blood can supply more oxygen and food to the muscles that need them.

Heart diseases

Sometimes the heart goes wrong. Some of the commonest diseases of middle-aged and elderly people are heart diseases. Smoking and too much fat in the diet can damage the arteries, which puts a great strain on the heart. It has to squeeze the blood harder to get it through narrowed arteries. This harder squeeze is what we call high blood pressure. High blood pressure can usually be lowered by medicines, but in very serious cases heart surgery may be necessary.

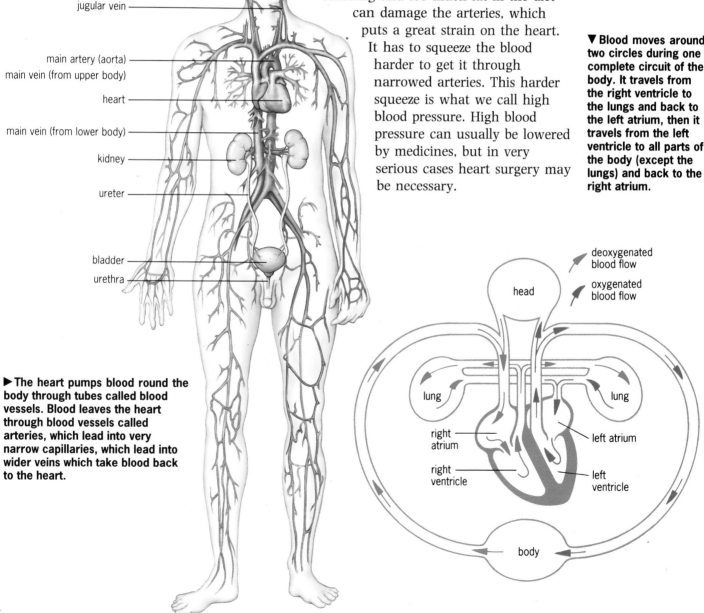

head artery
jugular vein

main artery (aorta)
main vein (from upper body)

heart

main vein (from lower body)

kidney

ureter

bladder
urethra

▶ The heart pumps blood round the body through tubes called blood vessels. Blood leaves the heart through blood vessels called arteries, which lead into very narrow capillaries, which lead into wider veins which take blood back to the heart.

▼ Blood moves around two circles during one complete circuit of the body. It travels from the right ventricle to the lungs and back to the left atrium, then it travels from the left ventricle to all parts of the body (except the lungs) and back to the right atrium.

deoxygenated blood flow

oxygenated blood flow

head

lung

lung

right atrium

left atrium

right ventricle

left ventricle

body

Blood

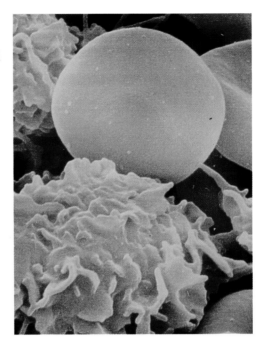

▶ Greatly magnified photograph of white blood cells, red blood cells and platelets. The two large rough-surfaced objects are white cells which engulf and digest foreign materials entering the body. The small spiky objects are platelets which help blood to clot.

A drop of blood contains about 100 million red blood cells. More than 2 million red blood cells are destroyed and replaced every second.

The blood of lobsters is pale blue, as oxygen is carried by haemocyanin which contains copper and not haemoglobin.

▼ Your body has a puncture repair kit. When you bleed, tiny objects called platelets send out fibres which trap red cells. Blood then changes into a thick jelly, a blood clot, which blocks the wound.

Most animals have blood inside them. Only some of the smallest and simplest animals, such as corals and flatworms, do not have any. All animals with backbones (vertebrates), and most of those without (invertebrates), have some sort of blood system. These do not all function in the same way.

The blood of vertebrates is made up of a fluid, called plasma, with blood cells floating in it. These blood cells do a number of different jobs. They may carry oxygen, help blood to clot, produce antibodies or eat invading bacteria.

The blood is pumped through tubes (blood vessels) round the body by a muscular pump, the heart. Blood acts as a transport system for carrying materials to places where they are needed. It takes dissolved foods such as glucose sugar from the intestines to all parts of the body. It also carries wastes, including urea and carbon

dioxide, from all the body organs. Urea is removed from the blood in the kidneys as urine is made. The gas carbon dioxide passes out of the blood into the lungs and is breathed out. Hormones, the chemical messengers that control a number of functions, such as growth, are also transported in the blood.

The blood of vertebrates (like ourselves) is usually red. It is red because of a coloured protein called haemoglobin found in red blood cells. This can carry oxygen. Blood carries oxygen from the lungs to all the cells of the body.

Blood can defend us from damage and infections in at least three quite different ways. First, it can seal up cuts or other damage to the skin because it is able to set (clot) quickly. This patching stops the escape of more blood and prevents dirt and germs from entering. Secondly, special white blood cells called lymphocytes make antibodies. Antibodies recognize germs invading the body and attach to them. The germs are then easily picked out and destroyed by other defences. Thirdly, other white blood cells, called phagocytes, destroy germs by eating them.

There are a few rare diseases that stop the proper working of the blood, such as haemophilia and leukaemia. Haemophilia is an inherited disease. The blood of a haemophiliac does not clot normally. Leukaemia is a type of blood cancer. It happens when the body makes too many of one or other type of blood cell. Choked with these extra cells, the blood cannot function as it should.

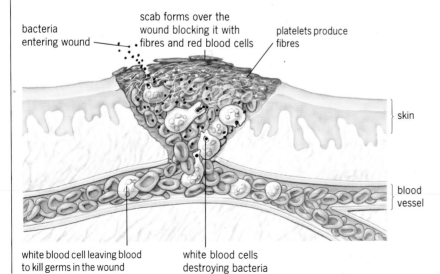

bacteria entering wound

scab forms over the wound blocking it with fibres and red blood cells

platelets produce fibres

skin

blood vessel

white blood cell leaving blood to kill germs in the wound

white blood cells destroying bacteria

The liver and kidneys

Liver

All animals with backbones have a liver. In adult humans it weighs over a kilogram (2½ lb), is reddish brown in colour and stretches all the way across the body just above the waist.

The liver receives blood full of digested food from the gut. It stores some foods, such as vitamins, minerals and glucose sugar. It takes the goodness out of unwanted proteins, storing it as carbohydrate or fat, and changes what is left into a harmless waste, called urea, which is removed by the kidneys.

The liver can also change some poisons from germs, alcohol and drugs into harmless substances. It makes the chemical needed to clot blood in wounds, and the bile needed to digest fats and oils. All these processes make a lot of heat, which the blood carries around the body to keep it warm.

Kidneys

All fish, amphibians, reptiles, birds and mammals have kidneys. They filter blood to remove waste products and excess water. The liquid waste that results is called urine.

Humans have two bean-shaped kidneys attached towards the back of the body just above the waist. Each one is joined to the bladder by a tube called a ureter. Urine passes down the ureters to the bladder before being passed out of the body by urination.

High-pressure blood comes to the kidneys through the renal arteries. It passes into millions of tiny tubes called nephrons, where waste products are filtered out as urine. The blood leaves the kidneys by the renal veins. By removing water, salts and waste products the kidneys are responsible for 'cleaning' the blood and maintaining its balance.

Your kidneys filter your blood 50 times a day.

If one kidney stops working the other will enlarge and do the work of two.

▼ A kidney cut in half. Kidneys are part of the body's waste disposal system. They filter blood to stop your body being poisoned by its own wastes.

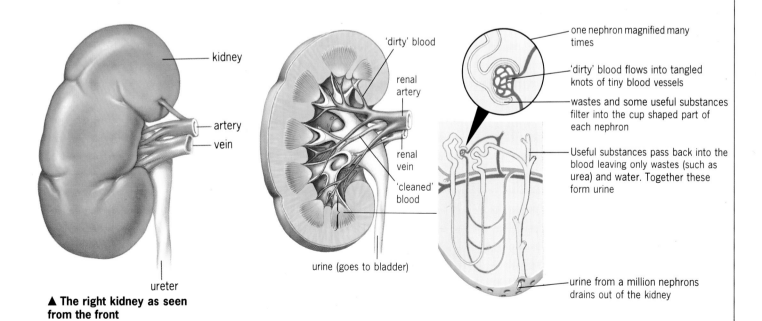

kidney

artery

vein

ureter

▲ The right kidney as seen from the front

'dirty' blood

renal artery

renal vein

'cleaned' blood

urine (goes to bladder)

one nephron magnified many times

'dirty' blood flows into tangled knots of tiny blood vessels

wastes and some useful substances filter into the cup shaped part of each nephron

Useful substances pass back into the blood leaving only wastes (such as urea) and water. Together these form urine

urine from a million nephrons drains out of the kidney

Digestion

The digestive system of an animal breaks its food down into liquid. The gut is a long tube that stretches from the mouth to the anus.

You chew food to break it into small pieces which are easy to swallow. Your front teeth bite off a chunk. Then your tongue pushes it to your back grinding teeth. These break up food and mix it with saliva. Saliva is produced by the salivary glands. It softens the food and begins to digest it. When the food is well chewed you swallow it.

The chewed food then passes down the gullet (oesophagus) to the stomach. It is pushed through the gut by muscular squeezing called peristalsis. In the stomach it is churned up and mixed with acid and digestive juices called enzymes. The acid and digestive enzymes kill any bacteria in the food and help to break it down into smaller substances which will dissolve in water. This enables the food to pass easily through the gut wall into the blood.

Your small intestine is over 6 m long and, because of its villi, has an inside surface area of 10 sq m. There are about 40 villi in each square millimetre of small intestine.

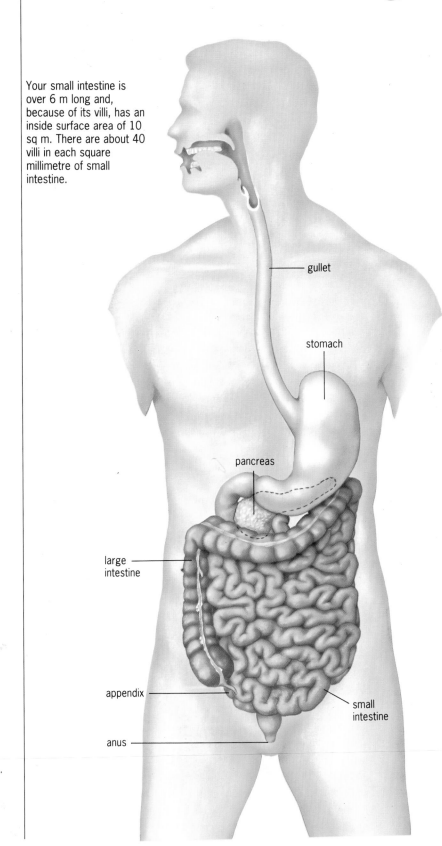

gullet

stomach

pancreas

large intestine

appendix

anus

small intestine

SWALLOWING

Food is moved along the gullet to the stomach by circular muscles. These muscles squeeze together (contract) behind the food, and relax in front of the food so that it is pushed along. The food moves forwards at about 20 cm a second.

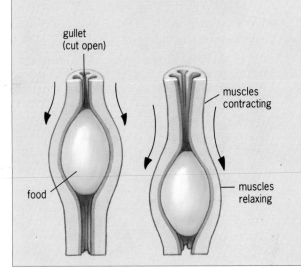

gullet (cut open)

muscles contracting

food

muscles relaxing

Partly digested food is passed from the stomach to the small intestine. Here digestion is continued by more digestive enzymes produced by the wall of the intestine and a gland called the pancreas. Digestion is helped by bile from the gall-bladder in the liver. Bile acts as a detergent, changing oily food into tiny droplets which are easier to digest.

The small intestine is lined with a carpet of tiny, finger-shaped bumps called villi. These give the intestine a huge surface area. Through it digested (liquid) food, along with vitamins, minerals and water, is taken into the blood. The blood system carries it first to the liver, and then to all parts of the body, to provide energy and materials for growth and repair.

The parts of food which cannot be digested, such as fibre from vegetables and fruit, pass into the large intestine. The large intestine is made up of the colon, rectum and anus. The undigested food remains in the colon for between 12 and 36 hours. Water and salt are removed from it during this time. It passes into the rectum and out of the anus as faeces.

ABSORPTION

A carpet of villi 1 mm high lines the small intestine. These give the intestine a huge surface area for absorbing digested food.

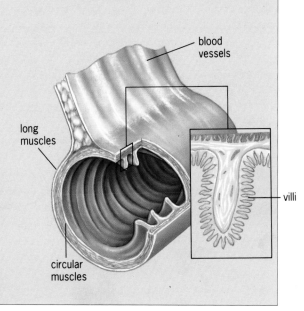

	Kilojoules per 100 g	Types of food
meat and fish	600 to 1,200 kJ	Mostly protein with a lot of fat and oil. Many vitamins, especially in fish oil.
dairy produce	300 to 3,000	Mostly fat, especially butter and cheese. Eggs have a lot of protein and many vitamins.
cereals	1,000 to 1,600	Mostly starchy carbohydrate with a little protein. Some vitamins in wholemeal bread.
vegetables	40 to 350	Contain a lot of water, some carbohydrate and protein. Very little fat. Very rich in vitamins.
fruit	100 to 300	Contain a lot of water with some carbohydrate and a little protein. Rich in vitamin C.
sweets and cakes	1,000 to 2,300	Mostly carbohydrate, especially sugar, with some fat and a little protein. No vitamins.

Food

Food supplies you with energy, and with the materials your body needs for growth, repair of wounds, wear and tear, and staying healthy.

Foods are mixtures of useful nutrients, together with things that the body cannot use. There are five types of nutrient: carbohydrates, fats, proteins, vitamins and minerals. These nutrients are absorbed into the blood during digestion.

Carbohydrates and fats give you energy. Proteins are used in growth and repairing damaged body parts. Vitamins and minerals have many different functions and are essential to good health.

▲ The energy supplied by food is measured in units called kilojoules (kJ). Different foods supply different amounts of energy, as the food chart shows.

Breathing

Adult human lungs can hold a total of 5 litres of air. But in normal breathing only half a litre of air is breathed in and out.

Adult lungs have an internal area of over 90 square metres, that is about half the area of a tennis court. This whole area is covered with a net of tiny blood vessels (capillaries) which, if joined end to end, would reach from London to New York. Each day you breathe about 13,500 litres of air into your lungs.

Like most land animals, people breathe air. Breathing has to go on all the time for you to stay alive. Every minute you breathe in about twelve times and breathe out about twelve times. Breathing is the forcing of air in and out of the lungs. Your lungs are in your chest and are connected to the back of your throat by a tube called the windpipe. Air moves in and out of the windpipe through your mouth or nose.

You breathe in by making your chest bigger so that air is sucked into your lungs. This happens when muscles pull your ribs upwards and outwards, and a sheet of muscle below the lungs, called the diaphragm, is pulled downwards. You breathe out by lowering your ribs and raising your diaphragm.

We breathe all the time because our bodies need a constant supply of the gas called oxygen. We use oxygen to gain energy from our food. We, and other land animals, get oxygen from the air. Fish use their gills to extract the oxygen which is dissolved in water. Oxygen in the air you breathe passes into the red blood cells in the blood vessels of your lungs. At the same time the waste gas carbon dioxide passes from your blood into your lungs and is breathed out.

Our brains control the speed of our breathing. This is to provide enough oxygen at all times for the body's needs. When you are quiet and still, perhaps asleep, your energy needs are low; you require little oxygen and your breathing is slow and shallow.

If you start exercising hard, say running 200 m (650 ft) as fast as you can, you need much more energy. Without thinking about it you automatically find yourself breathing faster and more deeply.

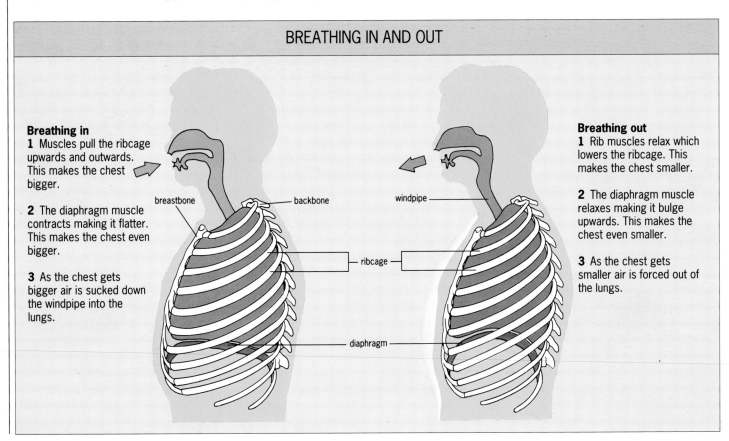

BREATHING IN AND OUT

Breathing in
1 Muscles pull the ribcage upwards and outwards. This makes the chest bigger.

2 The diaphragm muscle contracts making it flatter. This makes the chest even bigger.

3 As the chest gets bigger air is sucked down the windpipe into the lungs.

breastbone — backbone — windpipe

ribcage

diaphragm

Breathing out
1 Rib muscles relax which lowers the ribcage. This makes the chest smaller.

2 The diaphragm muscle relaxes making it bulge upwards. This makes the chest even smaller.

3 As the chest gets smaller air is forced out of the lungs.

Lungs

Lungs are organs where oxygen is extracted from the air and carbon dioxide is extracted from the blood. Usually there is some means for pumping air in and out of the lungs so that this exchange of gases can happen quickly. This is called breathing.

All mammals, birds, reptiles and air-breathing amphibians have lungs. In all of these the lungs develop during early growth as a pair of pockets that grow out from a front part of the gut. This is why all these animals breathe through their mouths and noses. In mammals and birds the lungs are found inside the chest, protected by the rib cage. Air gets to and from the lungs via the trachea (windpipe) that opens into the gut in the throat.

Breathing happens when the lungs are expanded and squeezed by movements of the rib cage and of the diaphragm under-neath them.

The inside surface of the lung is folded to form thousands of tiny air-filled pockets called alveoli. The oxygen passes from these into nearby blood capillaries, and the waste gas carbon dioxide passes out from the blood into the air to be breathed out.

Birds have lungs designed to give them a rapid supply of air when their muscles are working very hard during flying. Most species of fish do not have lungs. One species that does is called the lungfish. Their lungs are filled with air when they put their noses through the water surface. They also have gills for underwater.

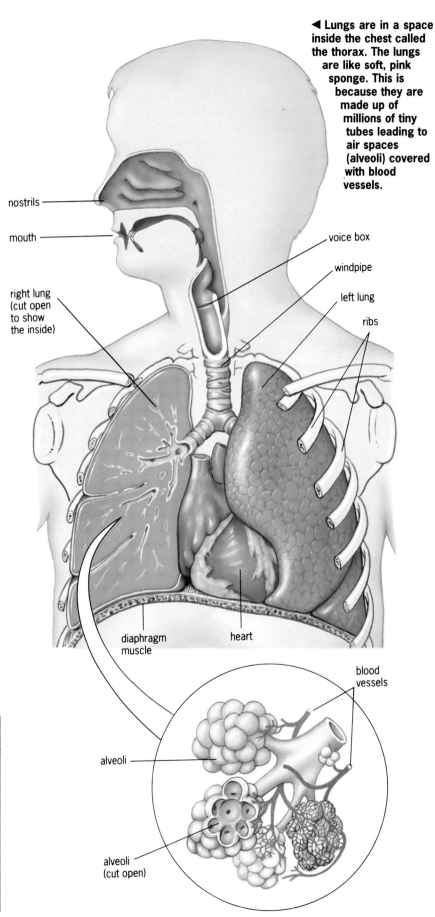

◀ Lungs are in a space inside the chest called the thorax. The lungs are like soft, pink sponge. This is because they are made up of millions of tiny tubes leading to air spaces (alveoli) covered with blood vessels.

nostrils

mouth

voice box

windpipe

right lung (cut open to show the inside)

left lung

ribs

diaphragm muscle

heart

blood vessels

alveoli

alveoli (cut open)

RESPIRATION

All living things need energy. The 'fuel' which provides energy for living things is their food, and energy is released from food by a process called respiration. Sugar and fats in food are combined with oxygen in a kind of controlled 'burning' in cells all over the body. This aerobic respiration releases energy plus water and carbon dioxide. In humans the oxygen needed for respiration is provided by the lungs. The lungs also get rid of the carbon dioxide gas that is produced as a waste product of respiration.

The brain

Many animals have a brain that controls their actions. The brain consists of many nerve cells. Each cell is connected to many other nerve cells, some of which pass information from sense organs, such as ears or eyes, into the brain, while others are connected to nerves that lead from the brain to muscles.

Most of the brain cells in mammals connect to other brain cells and process incoming information, carry out thought processes and make elaborate decisions. Even smaller and less intelligent animals, such as bees, can remember where their hive is and calculate the time of day.

There are about 100 billion cells in a human brain but only about 10,000 in that of an ant.

In humans, each of the 100 billion brain cells probably makes 1,000 connections to other nerve cells, so the total number of nerve connections is about 100 trillion.

Information from the senses

The sense organs pass information to different parts of the brain as a series of nerve impulses which act as signals. These may be simple signals, giving information about what part of the body has been touched, or a very complex series of signals using thousands of nerve cells to allow you to see the shape of the letters and read the words on this page.

Using information from different parts of the brain, an animal can send signals to its muscles so that it can move in a controlled way. Some types of movement, such as a single kick, do not require much control, but walking and flying require exact control of the muscles. You would fall over and bump into things if you could not adjust your muscles continually.

The brain receives and processes signals from the sense organs to make these adjustments. It connects with nerves in the spinal cord which runs down from the head, inside the backbone. Nerves from the spinal cord connect with muscles, while other nerves from sense cells in the skin and muscles connect back into the spinal cord. Other nerves connect the spinal cord back to the brain.

The human brain weighs about 1·5 kg (3 lb) and, for our body size, is far bigger than that of any other animal.

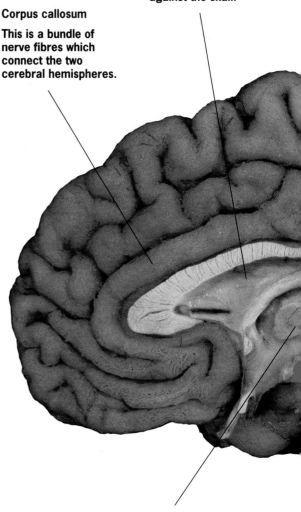

Ventricle

Tissues inside the ventricle produce cerebrospinal fluid. This fluid cushions the brain against the skull.

Corpus callosum

This is a bundle of nerve fibres which connect the two cerebral hemispheres.

Midbrain

This helps control eye movement.

▲ **Cross section of the human brain. An adult's brain would actually be about this size.**

Thinking and brain damage

Our brain allows us to think. We do not know exactly how this happens, but in humans the cerebral hemispheres are very large and are involved in consciousness, thought, recognition, memory and personality. If parts of the human brain are damaged, there is usually some loss of function or of mental ability. Damage to the cerebellar region of the brain may cause partial paralysis, as this part of the brain is involved in the control of the body's muscles. If your head is hit hard, parts of your brain may stop working for a while, causing unconsciousness and loss of memory.

The brain uses up one fifth of the oxygen used by the entire body when at rest. If the brain is starved of oxygen for more than three minutes serious damage is likely to occur.

Learning

Many animals with brains are able to learn. Animals with big, complicated brains are usually able to learn more than those with small brains. Having a large memory, based on life's experiences, allows an animal to make more complex decisions and generally to respond in a more intelligent manner. Humans, with their large brains and long memories, are probably the most intelligent animals. The brains of chimpanzees and other apes are also very well-developed, closely resembling the human brain. Whales and dolphins also have large, well-developed brains.

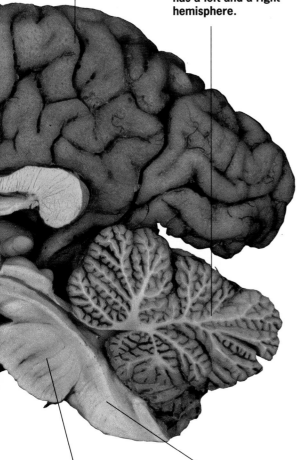

Cerebral hemisphere

These are involved in thought and memory; some parts respond to signals from the sense organs to allow sight, hearing, feeling, speech and movement.

Cerebellum

This is involved in balance and muscle co-ordination. Like the cerebral hemispheres it has a left and a right hemisphere.

Medulla oblongata

This controls breathing, heart beat and blood pressure. It also helps control swallowing, sneezing, coughing and vomiting. Damage to this part of the brain usually results in death.

Spinal cord

Nerves arising from spinal cord connect with many different parts of the body. Humans have 31 pairs of spinal nerves.

MEMORY

Memory is the ability to recall things and feelings from the past. Scientists are still a long way from understanding how memory works. What is known is that memory about events long ago and memory of things that have just happened are controlled by different parts of the brain.

Part of the action of storing a memory seems to be the making of new links between nerve cells in the brain. It is easier to remember things if you repeat them many times, or if they are very unusual or unpleasant.

After an accident or a shock some people lose their memories. This is called amnesia, and is usually only temporary.

Nervous systems

If you imagine that the body of an animal is a living machine, then the nervous system is the machine's controls. It ensures that all the parts of an animal's body are co-ordinated and that the animal responds

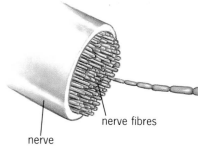

nerve fibres

nerve

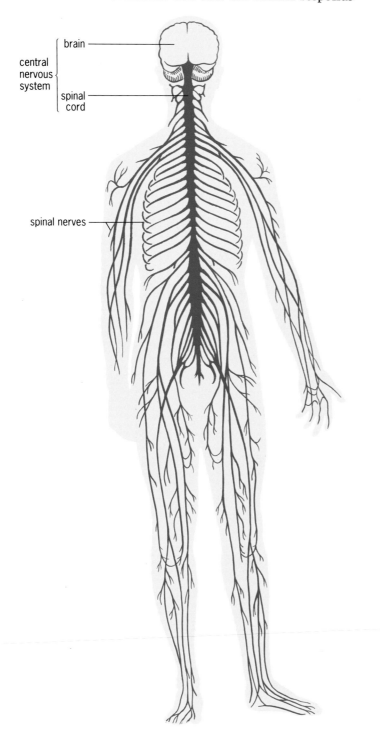

central nervous system

brain

spinal cord

spinal nerves

to any changes in its surroundings, such as being chased by a predator or a drop in temperature. All backboned animals have a nervous system made up of three main parts: the brain, the spinal cord and the nerves.

Central nervous system

The brain and the spinal cord make up what is called the central nervous system. This is protected by bone: your brain by your skull and your spinal cord by your backbone. The central nervous system is connected to all other parts of your body by nerves.

Peripheral nervous system

This is made up of the nerves that connect all the parts of your body with your brain and spinal cord. The nerves carry electrical messages (nerve impulses). Sensory nerves carry information from your sense organs, such as your eyes, ears, nose, taste buds, and touch sensors in your skin, to your brain. The brain interprets this information and sends out nerve impulses through the motor nerves. The motor nerves carry nerve impulses from the brain to the part of the body where action is needed, such as a muscle or a gland.

Nerve cell structure

Nerves are made up of bundles of nerve fibres. Each of the thousands of nerve fibres is a nerve cell. Nerve cells, like other cells, consist of a nucleus surrounded by

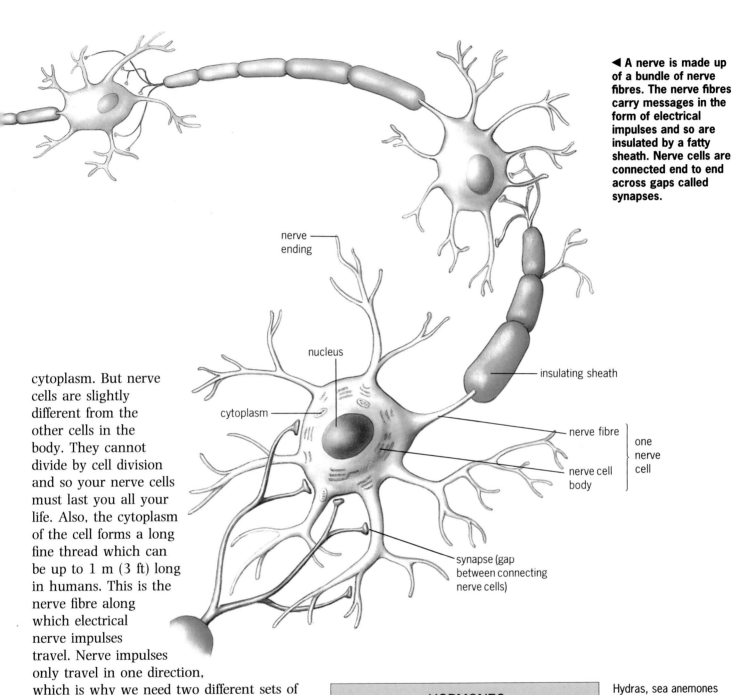

◀ A nerve is made up of a bundle of nerve fibres. The nerve fibres carry messages in the form of electrical impulses and so are insulated by a fatty sheath. Nerve cells are connected end to end across gaps called synapses.

nerve ending

nucleus

cytoplasm

insulating sheath

nerve fibre

nerve cell body

one nerve cell

synapse (gap between connecting nerve cells)

cytoplasm. But nerve cells are slightly different from the other cells in the body. They cannot divide by cell division and so your nerve cells must last you all your life. Also, the cytoplasm of the cell forms a long fine thread which can be up to 1 m (3 ft) long in humans. This is the nerve fibre along which electrical nerve impulses travel. Nerve impulses only travel in one direction, which is why we need two different sets of nerves.

Reflexes

Reflexes are actions which you do without having to think about them. They are built into your nervous system. Reflexes include pulling your hand away if you touch something hot, and your mouth watering when you smell food.

HORMONES

Nervous system control in animals is good for rapid, precise actions. Animals also use a slower chemical control system for activities that happen over longer periods, such as growth and reproduction. This chemical control is based on chemical messages called hormones. They are produced by glands and circulate round the body, mainly in the blood. Plants also produce hormones, such as auxins which control growth.

Hydras, sea anemones and jellyfish have a simple nervous system made up of nerve cells connected together to make a net.

Eyes

▶ **The diagram shows the internal structure of an eye. Nerve cells pass messages to the brain. The image at the back of the eye is upside-down. The brain interprets it the right way up.**

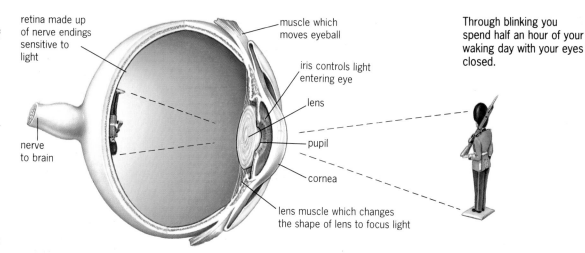

retina made up of nerve endings sensitive to light

nerve to brain

muscle which moves eyeball

iris controls light entering eye

lens

pupil

cornea

lens muscle which changes the shape of lens to focus light

Through blinking you spend half an hour of your waking day with your eyes closed.

Each of your eyes contains about 142 million light-sensitive nerve endings, 10 million of which are sensitive to colour. You can see objects as small as 0.1 mm (0.004 in) across and tell the difference between 10 million different colour shades.

▲ **The short-eared owl has large eyes. At night, when they are actively searching for prey, the pupils collect as much light as possible.**

▶ **The compound eyes of insects vary from huge ones like these eyes of a horsefly with their thousands of facets, to the tiny eyes of some ants which have about a dozen facets.**

An eye is a living camera. It focuses light from surrounding objects to form a picture which can be understood by the brain. Humans, and other animals with backbones, have eyes built in the same way.

At the front of the eye is a clear, round window called the cornea. Tears from tear glands keep it moist and clean and, together with the eyelids and eyelashes, help protect it from damage. The cornea, and the lens behind it, focus light onto a layer of sensory cells at the back of the eye called the retina. The pictures focused on the retina are detected by its sensory cells, which send messages along nerves to the brain which are converted into sight.

Just behind the lens is a sheet of muscle, called the iris. This is the coloured part of the eye. It has a round hole at its centre called the pupil. In bright light the iris muscles contract and make the pupil smaller to stop too much light entering the eye. In dim light the muscles relax and the pupil opens to let in more light.

The most sensitive part of the retina is a patch of sensory cells, called the yellow spot, opposite the lens. Nerve messages from our eyes go to the brain, which uses them to give us a clear, moving, three-dimensional (solid), coloured picture of the outside world. This allows us to recognize things by their colour, shape and brightness. We need two eyes, because with only one eye it is difficult to judge distance and depth.

Animals' eyes

Animals such as owls, cats and bush-babies, which are active at night, have very large pupils to gather as much light as possible. In daytime their pupils are very small. Insects and crustaceans have eyes quite different from ours. They are made up of hundreds or even thousands of narrow light-sensitive tubes. Each one cannot make a proper picture, but together they can. These are called compound eyes.

Ears

All mammals have ears. Bats have large ears that act rather like radar aerials. Flying bats at night make high-pitched sounds that are too high for humans to hear. These sounds bounce off flying insects, such as moths, like a radar beam. The returning echoes are picked up by the bat's big ears so that it can find and catch the insect in mid-air. Some prey animals like rabbits and hares have big ears so that they can hear their enemies approaching and tell which direction they are coming from. Birds, reptiles and amphibians have good hearing, but their ears are simpler than those of mammals. Some insects can also hear, but their ears may be placed on their front legs or the sides of their bodies. Insect ears are very simple, consisting only of a thin membrane. When sound waves strike the membrane it vibrates.

◀ The fennec fox lives on African savannahs (grasslands). It has huge, movable ears that let it accurately find sounds of insects like termites underground. It then digs them up and eats them.

Structure of the human ear

The part of the ear that you can see is called the outer ear. As it is funnel-shaped, it collects sound waves and focuses them on the eardrum inside the head. The eardrum then vibrates, which causes the group of tiny bones (ossicles) that are attached to it to vibrate as well. The ossicles act as levers to increase the force of the vibrations moving the liquid in the snail-shaped inner ear called the cochlea. Inside this, sensitive hair cells are moved by the vibrations. As these are attached to nerves, every time they are vibrated messages are sent to the brain. These nerve messages enable us to hear and understand sounds, including speech.

The ear and brain working together can separate sounds depending on how loud they are and how high or low they are. Having two ears, one on each side of the head, helps us to tell where a sound is coming from, as it will be louder in one ear than the other unless it is straight ahead or immediately behind.

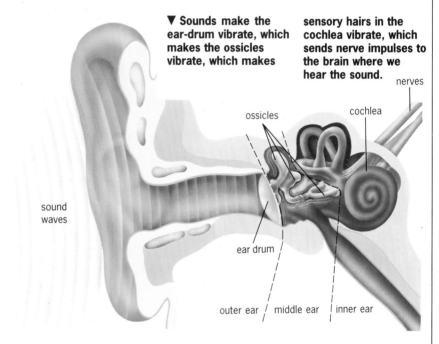

▼ Sounds make the ear-drum vibrate, which makes the ossicles vibrate, which makes sensory hairs in the cochlea vibrate, which sends nerve impulses to the brain where we hear the sound.

nerves

ossicles

cochlea

ear drum

outer ear / middle ear / inner ear

sound waves

Balance

Your sense of balance is controlled in your inner ear, where sense organs detect any change in the position of your head. You are probably not very aware of this, but without it you would be unable to move without falling.

Earache

This is the commonest illness of the ear. It is usually caused by an infection in the middle, hidden part of the ear. This region is connected by a tube (the Eustachian tube) to the throat. Bacteria can pass up the tube and cause infection and earache.

The lowest sounds humans can hear are at 20 vibrations a second (a low hum) and the highest are 20,000 vibrations a second (a high-pitched hiss). As you get older you are less able to hear the higher-pitched sounds. Very loud sounds, such as factory machinery, gun-fire or disco music, can damage the ears and cause deafness.

Noses

Most backboned animals have two nostrils. These are tubes running from the front of the head into the mouth. In mammals these tubes end in a special bulge called a nose.

The nose and its tubes have a number of important functions. They are a route for air to enter the lungs even when the mouth is shut or filled with food. A baby sucking at the breast can only breathe through its nose. The walls of the nostrils are usually lined with specialized sense cells which respond to odours that enter with breathed-in air.

An elephant's nose and upper lip, its trunk, has become another limb, with a grasping tip which can double as a hose-pipe. The nose of a whale, its blowhole, is on the top of its head, so it can breathe with its mouth under water. Most insects use their antennae as a 'nose'.

▶ Chemicals in the air you breathe dissolve in moisture-covered nerve ends in your nose. These chemicals make the nerves send messages to your brain which produces your sense of smell.

▼ The moth's antennae are its organs of smell, enabling it to find a mate.

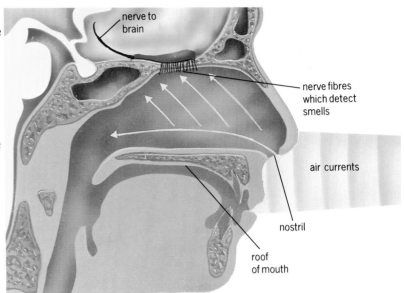

nerve to brain

nerve fibres which detect smells

air currents

nostril

roof of mouth

Smell

A sense of smell is very important to most animals. It is used to find food, a mate, and to avoid predators and the territories of other animals.

The sense of smell is closely linked to the sense of taste. Some of the substances you might think have a strong taste, such as chocolate and coffee, become unrecognizable if you are unable to smell them. High up in your nose is the olfactory organ. This is full of nerve fibres concerned with smell. Odours come from gas molecules released into the air. When these molecules are breathed in some dissolve in the mucous membrane lining your nose. These stimulate the smell receptors in the olfactory organ and a message is passed to the brain. This message is interpreted as a smell.

NOSEBLEEDS

Nosebleeds are usually nothing to worry about. They can occur if the lining of the nose becomes too dry. If you have a nosebleed, sit with your head forward over a bowl and pinch your nostrils closed. The bleeding should stop after about 10 minutes.

Skin and hair

Skin is our protective outer surface. It covers all the body and is made up of several layers. The lowest layer is living and makes all the other layers. The skin surface, called the epidermis, is made up of dead skin cells. It is kept supple by an oily substance made by the skin. The skin also removes sweat from the blood. Some skin cells contain a dark pigment called melanin. People with dark skins have more of these than people with light skins. These dark cells protect us from skin cancer, as they block the dangerous ultraviolet rays in sunlight. Most of the skin is covered with tiny hairs, which are made by the skin.

The functions of hair

The hairs on mammals have at least two important functions. The first is to do with controlling body temperature. Mammals have a high, steady body temperature. To be able to keep this up they have to make sure that heat does not escape from the body too fast. The hairs form a waterproof, insulating coat that slows down heat loss.

The second function of the hairs is to give an animal its characteristic markings. These are made out of hairs of different colours and lengths.

The structure of hair

We have very large numbers of individual hairs, tens of thousands on a head. Each hair, wherever you find it, grows out of a little pit in the skin called a hair follicle. The hair itself is dead and is made out of dead skin cells filled with a tough protein called keratin. Each hair does not last for ever. It grows for a while, perhaps for more than a year, and then naturally falls out and is replaced by a new one. As hair grows the skin coats it with a natural oil to protect it. We remove some of this oil by shampooing our hair.

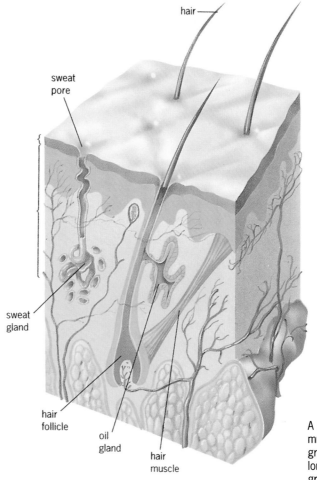

A hair grows about 12 mm in a month, but rarely grows more than 1 m long. Each hair usually grows for three to four years and is then pushed out by another growing from below. We have more body hairs than an ape, but our hair is so short and soft that we hardly notice it.

The colour of a hair, whether it is black, brown, reddish or blonde, is caused by different amounts of the colouring pigment called melanin. White hair has no melanin at all.

CURLY AND STRAIGHT HAIR

Under a microscope you can see the shape of a hair. Each hair grows from a hair follicle in the skin. The shape of these follicles determines how the hair grows so if you have round follicles your hair will always grow straight. Flat follicles will grow curly hair, and oval follicles wavy hair.

oval follicle
wavy hair

round follicle
straight hair

flat follicle
curly hair

Teeth

Most animals with backbones have teeth. They are used for holding, cutting and chewing food, so they have to be very strong. The part of a tooth that you can see is called the crown. Below the crown, hidden in the gums, is the tooth's root. This fixes the tooth firmly into the jawbone.

Most of the tooth is made of hard material called dentine. The crown is coated with an even harder material called enamel. Inside the tooth is a cavity filled with pulp. The pulp consists of blood vessels and nerve fibres.

▶ The root is attached to the jawbone by cement and tough fibres. The crown is protected by an outer layer of enamel, the hardest substance in the body.

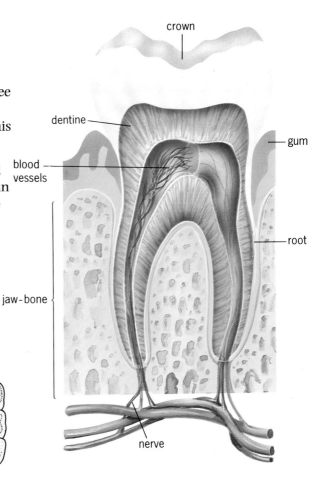

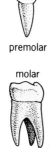

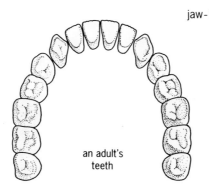

incisor canine premolar

molar

a child's milk teeth

an adult's teeth

▲ Teeth develop inside the jawbones before birth and first appear at about five months of age. By about six years children have 24 teeth. Twenty of these are milk teeth, and these fall out between seven and eleven years. They are replaced by 32 larger permanent teeth.

TOOTH DECAY

If you eat too much sugar and do not clean your teeth regularly you will get tooth decay.

Tooth decay occurs when small pieces of food, trapped in the teeth, are broken down by bacteria that live in the mouth. This produces acid which slowly damages the hard enamel coating the crown. Then it attacks the softer dentine, causing a hole or cavity. This results in toothache.

Apart from avoiding too much sugar, the best way to prevent tooth decay is by carefully brushing your teeth after every meal and before you go to bed.

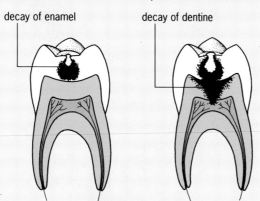

decay of enamel   decay of dentine

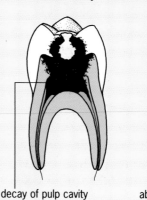

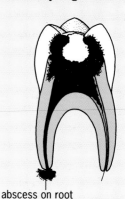

decay of pulp cavity   abscess on root

A baby is born with no teeth showing. Hidden in the gums are tiny growing tooth buds. The baby has two sets of buds. The most rapidly growing set are the first, or milk teeth. These appear during the first five years. Then they fall out and are replaced by the second, or permanent teeth. These should last all your life.

Special teeth

In most animals teeth are specialized for different jobs. Our upper and lower front four teeth have straight chisel-shaped ends. They are called incisors and are used for slicing mouth-sized pieces from food. On each side of the incisors is a single pointed tooth. This is the canine tooth. The canines are more developed in meat-eating animals and are used for puncturing the skin of their prey. Our back teeth, behind the canines, are broad-topped and bumpy. These are called molars. When you chew, you rub the upper and lower molars together, grinding up food into small pieces for swallowing.

In plant-eating animals the molars are large and have many ridges for grinding up large amounts of tough grass and leaf material. Meat-eating animals also have special molars for chewing meat with the sides of their jaws. The edges of these teeth slide past each other like blades of shears.

Going to the dentist

You should visit a dentist every six months to have your teeth checked. Dentists can treat tooth decay and gum disease at an early stage. They can also help to prevent these problems by thoroughly cleaning the teeth, and removing plaque and calculus, a hard, yellow substance caused by a build-up of plaque.

If you have a cavity in your tooth the dentist will fill it. First the tooth must be drilled to remove the decayed parts. The filling is put in place. It is usually made of silver amalgam, a mixture of silver, copper and tin. Once in place the filling is packed down and smoothed.

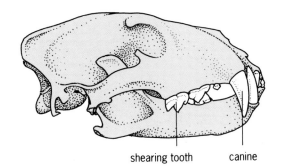

shearing tooth   canine

◄ Lion (carnivore) Carnivores have long canines to kill prey, and hold onto them. Massive shearing teeth crack bones and cut flesh.

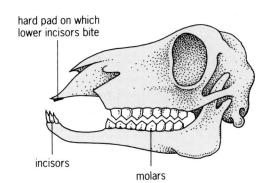

hard pad on which lower incisors bite

incisors

molars

◄ Sheep (herbivore) Herbivores cut grass by moving their chisel-edged lower incisors sideways across a thick pad on the upper jaw.

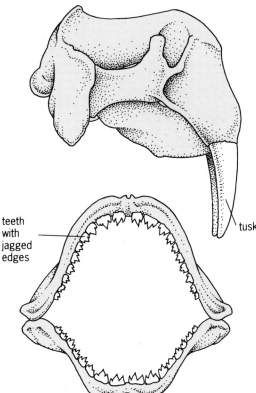

teeth with jagged edges

tusk

◄ Walrus (carnivore) A walrus uses its huge, tusk-like upper canines to defend itself and to compete against other walruses. In a herd it is the largest walrus with the largest tusks who is dominant.

◄ Shark (carnivore) The jagged teeth cut through flesh like a chainsaw and hold prey firmly in the mouth. Unlike mammals most fish have teeth that are all similar.

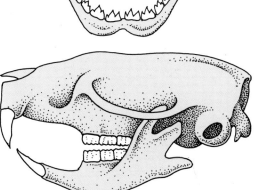

◄ Rat (herbivore) Rats are rodents and all rodents have long incisors with sharp edges, like chisels, for gnawing.

Reproduction

▲ The male frog clasps the female tightly, and as she lays her eggs into the water, he releases his sperm to fertilize them.

As all living things will eventually die, they must all also reproduce. Living things produce young like themselves: lions do not give birth to leopards; acorns will grow only into oak trees. This happens because the genes, the chemical instructions for making a living thing, are passed from one generation to the next during reproduction.

Sexual reproduction

Many living things reproduce sexually. All flowering plants have both a male part, the stamen, and a female part, the carpel. Pollen from the stamens fertilizes an ovule (the plant equivalent of an egg) in the carpels. The plant then produces seeds that grow into next season's plants.

Most animals reproduce sexually. The male produces millions of tiny sperm, and the female produces fewer, larger eggs. One sperm joins with an egg, either in water around the parents (external fertilization) or

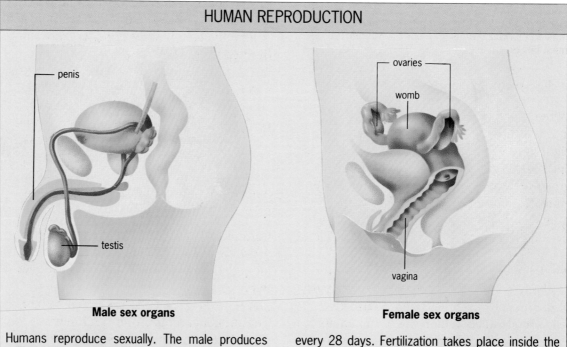

HUMAN REPRODUCTION

Male sex organs

Female sex organs

Humans reproduce sexually. The male produces millions of sperm cells in his testes each day. The female produces egg cells in her ovaries. One egg cell is released from one of the ovaries approximately every 28 days. Fertilization takes place inside the female's body. If the egg has been fertilized by a sperm, it attaches itself to the womb lining. Here it develops, over the next nine months, into a baby.

inside the female's body (internal fertilization). Most fish and frogs reproduce by external fertilization. Reptiles, birds and mammals reproduce by internal fertilization. Fertilization brings together genes from both parents and starts the development of a new animal.

▲ Only one of the millions of sperm cells which enter the female's body will suceed in fertilizing the much larger ovum.

Embryos and development

When an egg has been fertilized it splits into two; the two parts into four; four into eight; and so on. This turns the egg into an embryo: a growing ball of cells that gradually develops into a new animal. The embryos of many animals, including humans, look similar during early stages. In one group of mammals, the marsupials, young are born at a very early stage of development. Development continues in the mother's pouch. In fish, frogs, reptiles and birds the embryo develops from an egg, using food called yolk. Embryo mammals grow inside their mother's body using food from her blood. Development and growth of all animals continue even after the animal is no longer dependent on its mother.

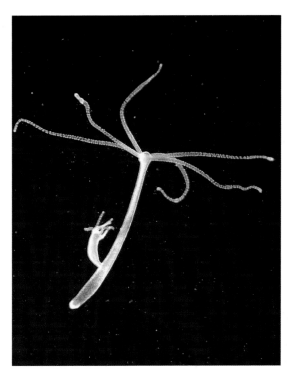

Budding and splitting

Some organisms reproduce without sex. This is called asexual reproduction and is found in both plants and animals. Amoebas are single-celled animals. To reproduce they simply split in two, and then the new cells grow to the size of the original cell and split again, and so on. Some animals with more than one cell can reproduce by splitting. Flatworms break up into two or more parts, and each part develops into a new adult. Some sea anemones, and their relatives like *Hydra*, can reproduce by budding. A small bud develops on the side of an adult and grows into a new animal joined to the parent by a stalk. Then the stalk breaks and there are two animals where before there was one.

Geraniums and many other plants can be grown from a cutting. A stem cut from a big plant grows roots and becomes a new young plant. Others, such as strawberry plants, send out long stems called runners. The runners produce roots and new growth. When the runners are separated from the parent plant new plants grow. These flowering plants are able to reproduce both sexually and asexually.

◄ Freshwater *Hydra* with bud. The bud is already catching its own food and will soon detach from its parent and become fully independent.

▼ This cutting from a plant stem has already grown roots. It will grow into a complete plant which is an exact copy of the parent plant.

Cells

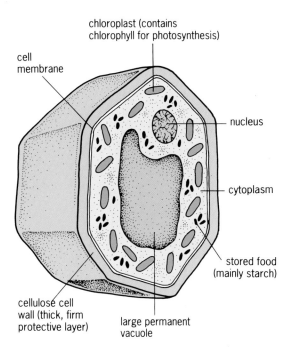

A typical plant cell. Plant cells are clearly visible under a microscope because they have a thick cellulose cell wall outside the much thinner cell membrane. Green chloroplasts, a nucleus and large vacuoles are clearly visible inside.

chloroplast (contains chlorophyll for photosynthesis)
cell membrane
nucleus
cytoplasm
stored food (mainly starch)
cellulose cell wall (thick, firm protective layer)
large permanent vacuole

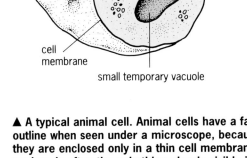

A typical animal cell. Animal cells have a faint outline when seen under a microscope, because they are enclosed only in a thin cell membrane. The nucleus is often the only thing clearly visible inside the cell.

stored food (oil droplets and glycogen – animal starch)
nucleus
cytoplasm
cell membrane
small temporary vacuole

Cells are the tiny, living building blocks from which microbes, animals and plants are made. Microbes and some very simple plants and animals, such as amoebas, have only one cell. Most living things are made of large numbers of cells all grouped together. Your body is made up of billions of cells. Most of them are very small and can only be seen with a powerful microscope. A red blood cell, for instance, is only 0·007 mm (0·0003 in) across.

Cell structure

Most cells have the same basic parts. They are each surrounded by a cell membrane which holds them together. Inside this membrane the cell is divided into two parts: the nucleus and the cytoplasm. The nucleus contains the body's genes. The genes, which are made up of DNA, control protein manufacture. These, and other chemicals, make all the substances in the body.

DNA

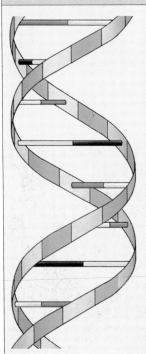

DNA (**D**eoxyribo**N**ucleic **A**cid) is a chemical substance found in every cell in every part of your body and it is responsible for what you look like and for making your body work properly.

DNA looks like a twisted ladder with each rung consisting of a pair of chemicals. It is a very long ladder, made of thousands of shorter ladders joined together. These shorter ladders, each with about 200 rungs, are called genes. Each gene carries a coded message that allows one type of protein to be made. The different proteins then determine every detail of your appearance: colour of hair and eyes; shape of nose and ears. The genes also contain the instructions needed to keep a cell working, whether it is in your liver, brain or blood.

Every cell in your body contains the same DNA but it is not found in a cell as one long twisted ladder. The DNA comes as 46 different ladders. Each of these DNA ladders is called a chromosome. 23 of these chromosomes are from your mother and 23 are from your father, which is why you may look like your parents.

The cytoplasm surrounds the nucleus and contains a number of different cell 'organs' called organelles. These have a range of functions. Some, the mitochondria, enable the cell to combine glucose with oxygen to provide an energy supply for the cell (respiration). Others, called ribosomes, make proteins. They receive chemical messages from the DNA in the nucleus which tell them exactly which proteins to make. In plant cells green organelles called chloroplasts contain the substance chlorophyll. This traps sunlight energy, which the chloroplasts use to build sugars from carbon dioxide and water (photosynthesis).

Tissues

Groups of cells are called tissues. The cells that make up a tissue are of the same type. So, for instance, muscle tissue consists of cells packed with a bundle of protein fibres that can shorten (contract). Nerve tissue consists of cells with long thin nerve processes and a cell membrane that can transmit electrical nerve impulses.

Cell division

Cells reproduce by dividing in two. The genes in the cell's nucleus are linked together in long threads called chromosomes. When a cell is ready to divide each chromosome splits in two. Now the cell has two copies of its genes (DNA). The nucleus and the cytoplasm then divide in half, forming two new cells each with a complete copy of the cell's DNA.

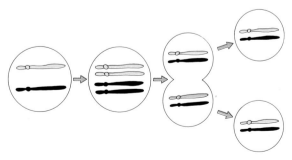

▲ **Each chromosome splits in two to form a second set of chromosomes. The cell itself then divides in two and each new cell receives a full set of chromosomes. All human cells, except the sex cells, contain 46 chromosomes and divide in this way.**

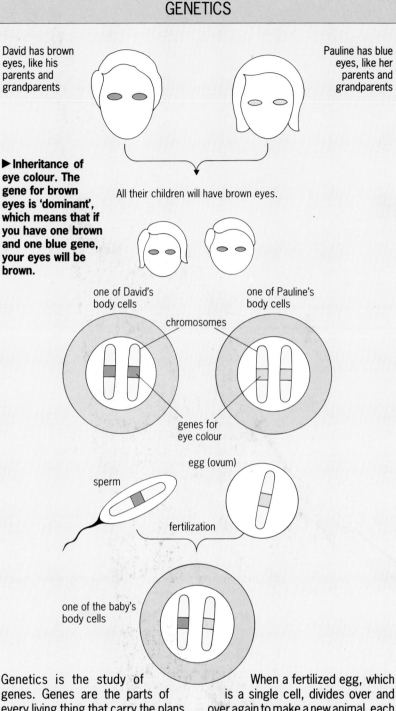

GENETICS

David has brown eyes, like his parents and grandparents

Pauline has blue eyes, like her parents and grandparents

All their children will have brown eyes.

▶ **Inheritance of eye colour. The gene for brown eyes is 'dominant', which means that if you have one brown and one blue gene, your eyes will be brown.**

one of David's body cells

one of Pauline's body cells

chromosomes

genes for eye colour

sperm

egg (ovum)

fertilization

one of the baby's body cells

Genetics is the study of genes. Genes are the parts of every living thing that carry the plans for making new organisms similar to the originals. The genes are made of DNA. They are arranged in lines on structures called chromosomes in the nucleus of each body cell. A human being has a set of 23 pairs of chromosomes in each cell, and each set contains tens of thousands of different genes. Each gene usually carries the code for making a different protein.

When a fertilized egg, which is a single cell, divides over and over again to make a new animal, each of the new cells receives an exact copy of the genes in the original egg. The fertilized egg contains half of the genes from the father's sperm, half from the mother. This means that the youngster that grows from the egg has a half-and-half mix of its parents' genes. This gene mix makes it grow into an animal of the same type as its parents and with some of the characteristics of both its mother and father.

Eggs

▶ **Hummingbird eggs weigh about one-fifth of the adult bird's weight.**

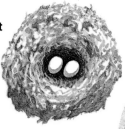

▶ **Ostriches lay up to ten eggs at a time, but several hens often lay them in one place, making a pile of as many as 50.**

▶ **Guillemot eggs are about 8 cm long and are laid on narrow cliff ledges. Their pointed shape makes them roll in a circle if knocked, rather than in a straight line over the cliff.**

▶ **The chick sits on a ball of food called yolk. This floats in a 'pond' of jelly, the egg white, which gives it moisture. The shell gives protection and lets in air.**

An egg is the cell made by a female animal which, when fertilized by a sperm, can grow into a new animal. Almost all animals have eggs. Most animals lay them in the outside world. They are normally covered with a protective layer of jelly or a tough shell. Fish eggs are laid in the sea or in lakes and rivers, turtle and crocodile eggs in the sand, frog eggs (frog-spawn) in ponds and birds' eggs in nests. All these eggs contain food in the form of yolk, which enables the young animal (embryo) to grow.

Most mammals, like ourselves, do not lay eggs. Instead they have tiny eggs without yolk, which are fertilized inside the mother's body. The embryo becomes attached to the mother's womb (uterus) by a placenta. This nourishes the growing baby, so that yolk food is not needed. Platypuses and spiny anteaters (echidnas) are the only mammals that lay eggs. Their eggs are soft-shelled, like those of snakes and lizards.

How bird eggs are made

A bird's egg has many layers. It has a hard shell on the outside for protection, which lets oxygen pass inwards. Inside is a membrane, and inside that the white. This is a store of water and protein food. Right in the centre of the egg is the yolk, made of fat and proteins to feed the growing chick.

Inside a mother bird the parts of an egg are put together from the inside outwards. An egg starts as a large, yolky cell (an oocyte) in the bird's ovary. It breaks free and passes along a tube called an oviduct, where it is fertilized. The fertilized oocyte is the egg's yolk, and on its surface the embryo begins to grow. Moving down the tube, the yolk is covered by white, then by the membrane, and finally by the shell itself.

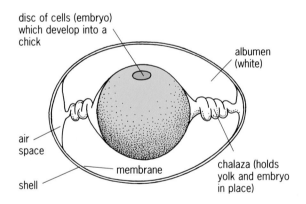

When an egg is laid, the young bird inside continues to grow using the yolk and white as food. It needs to be kept warm all the time, and the parents manage this by taking turns sitting on eggs in the nest. This is called incubation. At the end of incubation the bird hatches by breaking out of the egg. Incubation can take eleven days for small birds such as sparrows, and 80 days for the largest birds, such as ostriches.

Growth

All living things are able to grow. Food is essential for growth, but the foods needed are different for plants and animals. Plants need only carbon dioxide gas from the air, water and mineral salts from the soil, and sunlight, for growth.

Animals need water too. But they also need many complicated foodstuffs like starches, proteins, fats and vitamins. These they can get only by feeding on the bodies of other animals and plants.

Although the foods used are different, the ways in which animals and plants grow are similar. To get bigger, living things make more cells. They change the food they take in into the material for new cells. These are formed when the cells that are already present split in two (cell division). The faster this cell division goes on, the faster a plant or animal will grow.

When a baby grows into a child and then into an adult, this multiplication of cells occurs. Most of the organs of the body are made of cells that can increase in numbers and grow.

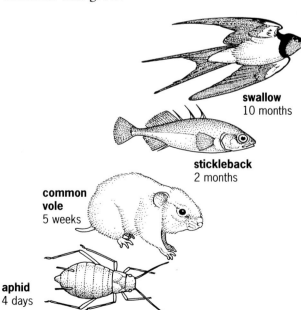

cicada
17 years

killer whale
10 years

chimpanzee
8 years

giant panda
4–5 years

frog
3 years

jackal
11 months

swallow
10 months

stickleback
2 months

common vole
5 weeks

aphid
4 days

◀ The time it takes for animals to reach the age at which they can breed varies enormously. Usually the larger an animal is, the longer it takes to grow up. One exception is the 17-year cicada, which spends a very long time as a larva.

Rates of growth

Animals grow at different speeds at different times of their life. A human grows fastest as a baby; the rate slows down after that, except for a growth spurt during puberty. Different parts of the body also grow at different rates. A baby's head grows more slowly than its legs and body after it is born.

In plants the cell division is concentrated at special growing points. These are usually at the tips of twigs or roots. In a bud, tiny new leaves and sections of stem are produced out of new cells. They are then expanded to full size when the cells are 'blown up' with extra water.

All changes in growth are under careful control so that the final shape and size of a growing animal or plant is as it should be. Growth is often controlled by hormones: chemical messages from glands that tell the body how much to grow.

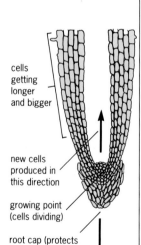

cells getting longer and bigger

new cells produced in this direction

growing point (cells dividing)

root cap (protects growing point)

root grows in this direction

▲ This diagram shows a slice through the tip of a plant root. Root growth is produced by a rapid division of cells just behind the tip.

Fungi

▲ **Fly agarics are found in birch and pine woods during autumn. They are poisonous and may grow to 16 cm in height.**

Over 100,000 species of fungi are known but it is thought that as many as 200,000 have yet to be discovered.

The hyphae of some rainforest fungi can spread for up to 500 m in the soil.

Moulds, mildews, yeasts and mushrooms are all fungi. Fungi live either on the dead remains of animals or plants, or as parasites on living things.

Yeasts have only one cell, but all other fungi are made of fine threads of cells called hyphae. These form a tangled mass called mycelium. Mushrooms are made up of interwoven hyphae and grow from a network of mycelium underground.

Fungi reproduce by making millions of microscopic spores in special reproductive hyphae. Mushrooms are reproductive hyphae. Each spore can make a new mycelium, which is why fungi are so common. Fungi grow so fast that a single spore can produce more than 1 km (²/₃ mile) of hyphae in 24 hours.

Decomposers

Fungi which decompose (rot) dead plants, animals and their wastes, break them down into chemicals which soak into the soil, keeping it fertile for plants.

▶ **Stag's horn fungus growing on an old tree stump. It is always found living on dead wood, growing to about 6 cm in height, at most.**

Disease carriers

Many fungi cause disease when they grow on living things. Athlete's foot is a fungus which infects skin between the toes, and farmer's lung fungus can infect vital organs causing serious harm. Rusts and smuts are fungi which cause plant diseases. In the 1840s a fungal disease called potato blight wiped out the Irish potato crop causing a million deaths from starvation, and a mass migration to the USA. Over 5,000 types of fungi attack crop and garden plants. Fungi can attack an incredible number of different materials: cloth, paint, leather, waxes, jet engine fuel, wire insulation, photographic film and even the coating of camera lenses.

Useful fungi

For centuries yeasts have been used in bread-making and brewing. A mould produces penicillin, which stops bacteria growing. This was the first antibiotic to be discovered. Other antibiotics are also produced by moulds.

Mushrooms are an important source of food for insects and many small animals. They are important in our diet too, being rich in B vitamins and iron.

Plants

Green plants are the only living things that are able to make their own food. They make food from water and carbon dioxide using the Sun's energy. This process, called photosynthesis, produces oxygen which is needed by living things for respiration. Animals rely on the food made by plants, either feeding on them directly or on other animals that do. Without plants all animals including humans would die.

How plants evolved

The first plants were single cells, floating in the oceans which covered the surface of the Earth. Eventually some cells formed clusters with special tasks, such as an anchor to keep the plant in place and a stalk to support the frond for photosynthesis and reproduction. Algae, the oldest group of plants, have remained this simple. When plants invaded the land they had to adapt to living in dry conditions unsupported by water; stems thickened and roots developed. The first land plants lived only in damp places, but today plants can be found growing almost everywhere from the edge of the Arctic ice to the hottest rainforests.

Colonizing new ground

The first plants to colonize new ground are lichens. They grow as a crust over the bare

◀ A slipper orchid. Orchids are one of the largest families of flowering plants in the world. They grow in all continents, except Antarctica, and in a wide range of habitats, from tropical forests to semi-deserts. Some species are very rare.

surface of rocks. When they die and rot their remains collect and form the first soil. Mosses grow in this, and their death and decay increases the amount of soil. Soon there is enough soil to support the growth of ferns and flowering plants. In this way a plant community develops, providing animals with food and creating a habitat.

Where plants grow

Botanists know of about 380,000 different species of plant, but most are found in the tropics. Of the 250,000 kinds of flowering plant 90,000 are found in Central and South America and 30,000 in tropical Africa. Further north the number decreases with only 1,800 species in Great Britain. The highest number of species in relation to area occurs in isolated places.

Plants have exploited nearly every environment on this planet but many are now at risk as their habitats are destroyed.

◀ Crustose lichens. There are about 20,000 species of lichen and though they can survive in extreme cold or where water is scarce, many cannot live where there is pollution.

Flowering plants

There are about 235,000 species of flowering plants. The smallest is a tiny duckweed called *Wolffia*, scarcely a millimetre across. The tallest is a type of eucalyptus tree which grows to over 100 m in height. These trees are so wide at their base that it would take ten people holding hands to encircle one.

Flowering plants are the most advanced and complicated group in the plant kingdom. They have flowers which contain sex organs that produce fruits and seeds. A seed is a tiny plant enclosed in a protective coat with a store of food so that, when conditions are right, it quickly forms a new plant.

Stems

Stems contain tubes which carry liquids around the plant. One set of tubes carries water and mineral salts from the soil to the leaves for photosynthesis. Other tubes carry liquid food, made in the leaves by photosynthesis, to the growing parts of the plant and to food storage organs such as tubers. Stems are usually stiff and upright, but some stay under-ground and may grow sideways through the soil. Stems may be hairy, spiny, smooth, furrowed, or rough, like tree bark.

Roots

Roots anchor a plant and absorb water and minerals from the soil. Fibrous roots consist of many fine branches which go out in all directions. Tap roots go straight down into the soil and may also store food. Carrots are tap roots.

Flowers

Flowers contain a plant's reproductive organs. The female part, the ovary, is in the centre and contains ovules which later become seeds inside a fruit. The male parts, the stamens, usually surround the ovary, although sometimes they are in a separate flower. They produce pollen grains to fertilize the ovule (pollination).

Fruit and seed

The fruit is the special part of a flowering plant in which seeds develop. Each fruit has evolved a special way to spread its seeds so the plant is successful. Some have tasty flesh so animals will eat them. Seeds are then spread in the animal's droppings. Other seeds have wings or hairy parachutes and are carried away by wind.

Leaves

Leaves need light to make food by photosynthesis, so they are arranged on the stem to receive as much light as possible. The veins of a leaf join up with the tubes running up and down the stem. Water is lost by evaporation from stomata (pores) on the leaf underside, so desert plants that must conserve water, such as cacti, often have very reduced leaves or spines.

◄◄ Bougainvillaea is a
South American shrub
which grows to about
3 m in height.

◄ All cactuses produce
flowers, but the flowers
may only last for a
couple of days, and
some flowers open only
at night.

Types of flowering plant

Flowering plants can survive in many
different places. Some grow in water,
which gives them more
support than air, so their
stems tend to be weak and
their leaves feathery. Shrubs
and trees are land plants
with tough, thick stems
made of wood. Non-woody
land plants, called her-
baceous plants, are
supported by water pressure
in their stems and leaves,
which is why they wilt in a
drought. Many desert plants
have leaves reduced to
tough, hard spines, and
thick fleshy stems full of stored water.
Some plants, such as mistletoe, are
parasites on other plants; some, such as
pitcher plants, have ways of catching
insects and a few, such as some tropical
orchids, sit high in tree branches with long
roots trailing to the ground.

The green chlorophyll in
leaves can use the energy
from sunlight to make
food materials out of
water and the carbon
dioxide gas in the air.

grow a new shoot, flowers
and seeds, then it dies
completely. **Perennial**
plants continue flowering
year after year. Each year
they make enough food to
produce fruits and seeds
with some to spare. This is stored for
growth next year.

◄ Waterlilies grow in
clear, shallow water.
The flowers grow on
long stalks rooted in the
mud bottom.

Life cycles of flowering plants

Each growing season a plant increases in
size and weight, and stores food until it has
enough to produce flowers and seeds.
Annuals are plants which are exhausted
after flowering and die, leaving only their
seeds to survive winter. **Biennials** have a
two-year life cycle. During the first year
they grow and make food, which is stored,
usually in the roots. The shoot dies but the
root survives winter underground. The
second year the plant uses this food to

first year	second year

◄ Annual plants have a
one-year life cycle.

◄ Biennial plants have
a two-year life cycle.

◄ Perennial plants
flower year after year.

Trees

oak tree in summer

▶The left half of the illustration shows an oak tree in the summer months when the twigs are covered in leaves. The right half of the same picture shows the tree in winter when the leaves have fallen and the branches and twigs look bare.

Trees are the largest land plants. Their strong, woody trunks support a mass of branches with buds producing leaves, the food factories of a tree. If you look at trees in winter you will see that some are bare and have lost their leaves. These are deciduous trees sometimes called the broadleaves. Others are covered with a mass of dark green foliage; these are the evergreens. Trees are giant forms of two main plant groups: the flowering plants and the conifers (conebearers).

Leaves

Leaves make food for the tree by providing a suitable site for photosynthesis. Light energy from the Sun powers this process, so each leaf needs to be in a position to receive the maximum amount of light. If you look up at a leaf canopy you will see the pattern made by the spreading leaves. They allow very little light to penetrate between them.

male flowers (catkins)

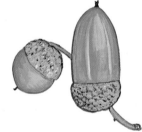

ovary

stigmas

female flowers, enlarged

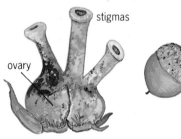

acorns

▲The male flowers of the oak are catkins which produce pollen. The female flowers have red stigmas to catch the pollen. After the ovary has been fertilized by the pollen, it swells and grows into an acorn.

Flowers and fruit

Acorns are the fruit of an oak tree, and its flowers dangle from new buds like yellowy-green catkins. Flowers appear in early May, before the leaves. Male and female flowers are separate: the male flowers are catkins; female flowers have three stigmas, and develop on spikes on buds at the end of a shoot. After wind pollination each ovary grows into an acorn, held in its own little cup.

Twigs

At the end of each twig and spaced along its length are buds. These will produce new leaves and flowers in the following season. Buds survive the harsh weather of winter so that the tree can grow again the next year.

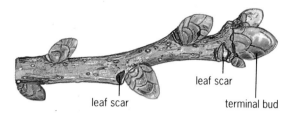

leaf scar

leaf scar

terminal bud

◄ **Twig from an oak tree in winter.**

Take the bud from the end of a twig and peel off each scale. These protect the tiny leaves and flowers in the middle. At the tip of each twig is a large terminal bud. This produces all the new growth that twig will make in the following season. Smaller buds beside it and along the length of the twig will grow into side shoots. On the stem below each bud is a crescent-shaped scar where a leaf was attached in the previous year.

Bark

Bark is the rough, grooved surface layer which covers the trunk and branches of a tree. It protects the living part of the tree's structure. New bark grows on the inside and dies as it gets pushed further out by later growth. As the girth of the tree increases, the rigid bark often cracks forming grooves.

Roots

Roots spread from the base of the trunk like underground branches. They have two basic functions. One is to form a secure anchor so the tree does not fall. The other is to absorb water and mineral salts from the soil. Roots are growing most of the time and only stop when it gets too cold. In some trees such as beech and birch the roots never grow very deep. Others like oak and pine are deeper rooting.

oak tree in winter

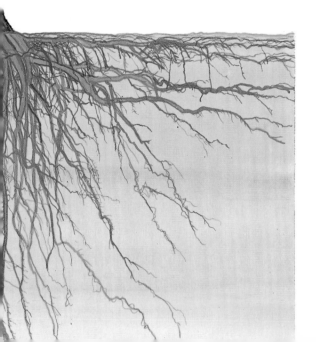

▼ **One way of recognizing different species of trees is by the patterns made by grooves in the bark.**

oak bark

ash bark

beech bark

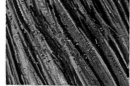

sweet chestnut bark

►Only a small part of a tree trunk is alive: a layer of dividing cells called the cambium which makes new bark and another layer of cambium which produces new sapwood and phloem each year. It is this second cambium which gives rise to annual rings.

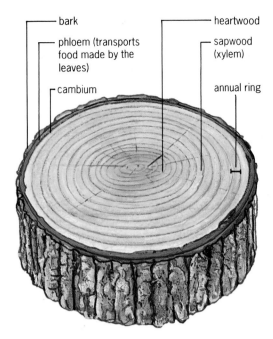

- bark
- phloem (transports food made by the leaves)
- cambium
- heartwood
- sapwood (xylem)
- annual ring

How a tree works

The water and mineral salts that the tree needs are carried by a system of tubes called the sapwood. Each season the tree produces new sapwood to carry sap to the buds ready for the new crop of leaves and flowers.

Working leaves continuously lose water by a process of evaporation called transpiration. Water, replacing that lost, moves up through the tree in a continuous column from the roots. Sap, carrying food made by the leaves, is transported down the tree in another set of tubes called the phloem. This food is taken to where it is needed or stored in the trunk or roots.

How trees grow

Trees increase in size as the branches and roots divide and grow longer spreading over a greater area. Trees also increase in girth, that is the diameter of the trunk and branches get larger each growing season.

Just inside the bark is a damp layer. This is one of the few living parts of the trunk, a layer called the cambium. Cambium cells are able to divide adding new wood cells (xylem) to the inside and new phloem to the outside. At the end of the season the sapwood cells are filled with waste products and become part of the dead centre of the tree, the heartwood. Bark is produced by another ring of cambium cells outside the phloem.

Growth rates

At the beginning of each season the cambium produces new sapwood. These large tubular cells supply water to the opening buds. As the season progresses, there is less need for new cells so fewer and smaller cells are produced. You can recognize these different rates of growth as the annual rings seen in the cut surface of a tree trunk or branch. The smaller, close-packed cells make a lighter coloured wood than the larger cells produced at the beginning of the season. In tropical countries the sapwood grows thicker throughout the year.

▼ Silhouettes of a selection of mature trees shown in winter.

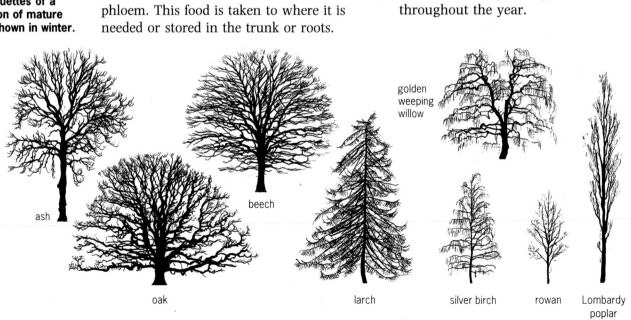

ash

oak

beech

larch

golden weeping willow

silver birch

rowan

Lombardy poplar

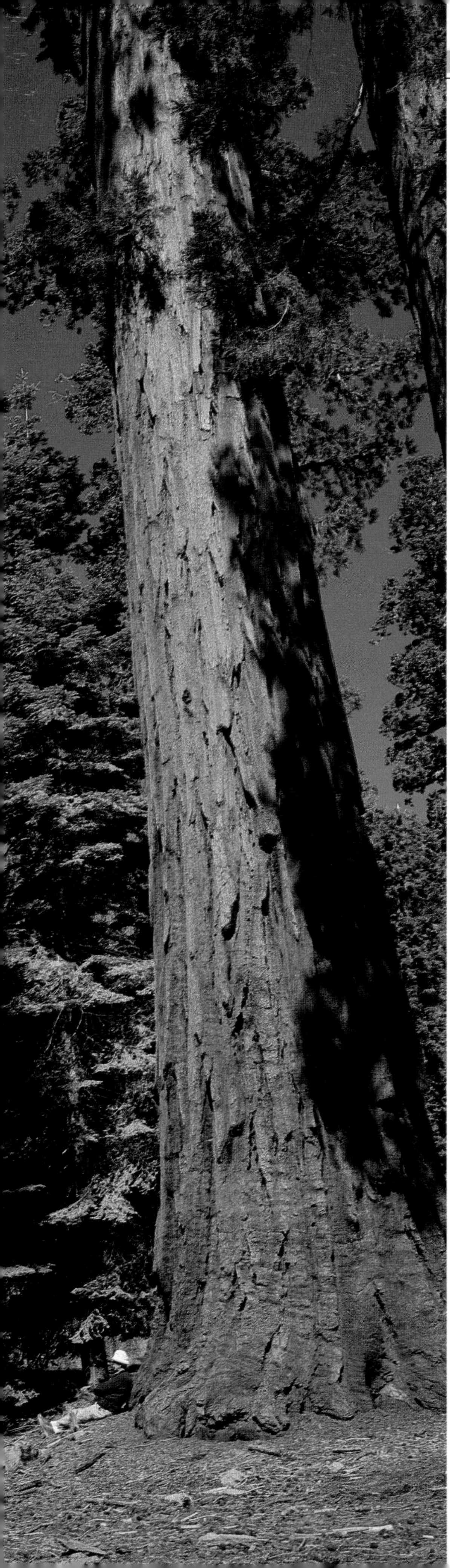

Hard and soft wood

Deciduous trees like oak, beech and ash are quite slow-growing. After 20 years they may only be 4 m (13 ft) high and reach a maximum of 13 m (43 ft) in 150 years. Conifers grow much more quickly reaching a height of 10 m (32 ft) in 30 years. Different rates of growth produce different types of timber. Slow growers have a denser wood called hardwood whereas fast growers produce a lighter timber called softwood.

1st year
young branch is cut at the 4th bud

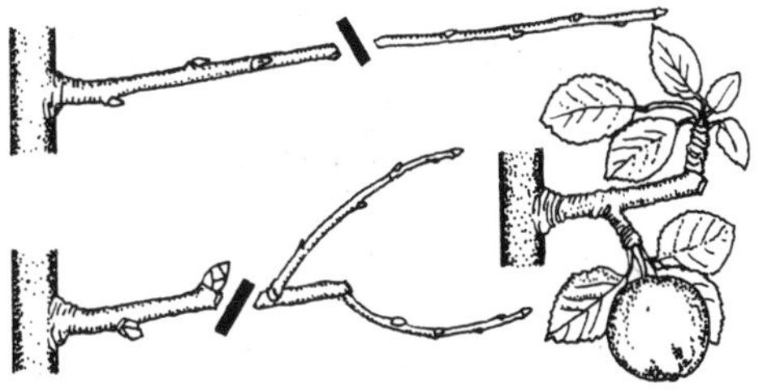

2nd year
branch is cut just after flower bud

3rd year
each bud produces a fruit

◀ **Apple and pear trees are pruned to increase their yield of fruit. By pruning away the growth buds, the flower buds develop and each produces a fruit.**

Pruning

This is the trimming of branches on fruit trees to encourage them to produce more flowering shoots and fruit. Some, like apples and pears, are trained against wires or a wall to form espalier or cordon fruit trees. These provide a large crop of fruit which is easy to pick. Topiary is a type of pruning in which evergreens, such as yew, are trimmed to form interesting shapes for decoration.

Giant conifers

Giant sequoias, like those in the photograph on the left, are conifers which grow in the mountains of California. They are not as tall as their close relatives the redwoods, which can grow over 90 m (300 ft), but their trunks are much larger.

The largest living tree is a giant sequoia called the 'General Sherman'. It is 83·8 m (274·9 ft) tall and measures 31·4 m (103 ft) around its base. As well as being the world's largest living thing it is also one of the oldest things on Earth, being between 2,200 and 2,500 years old.

◀ **Giant sequoias in the Mariposa Grove in Yosemite National Park, California, USA. The size of the person sitting by the tree gives an idea of the enormous girth and of the height of the trees.**

Grasses

Grasses are the biggest and most successful family of plants. They were the last group of flowering plants to evolve and survived when other plants had died out. Most grasses are herbaceous plants, which means they do not have woody stems and they die down to the ground after flowering. Many are annual: they live for a season, produce a large quantity of seeds and die. Each seed contains enough food for a new plant to grow. Cultivated grasses are called cereals. Wheat, maize, rice, sugarcane and bamboo are all members of the grass family. Whether ground into flour or cooked whole, grass seeds form the basis of the diet of humans all over the world. Wild grasses are are also the food of many animals too.

Grasses for food

Prehistoric people collected wild grain as a source of food and eventually realized that grain would grow better if it was planted in good soil and protected from wild animals. Over hundreds of years farmers selected and grew the better grain, so improving the overall quality. Archaeologists have found examples of cultivated grain in the country which is now Turkey. Farmers were planting and harvesting wheat and barley as long ago as 9000 BC.

Maize There are two main types of maize. One produces a head of large kernels known as sweet corn or corn on the cob. This is eaten fresh as a vegetable. The other

STRUCTURE OF A GRASS

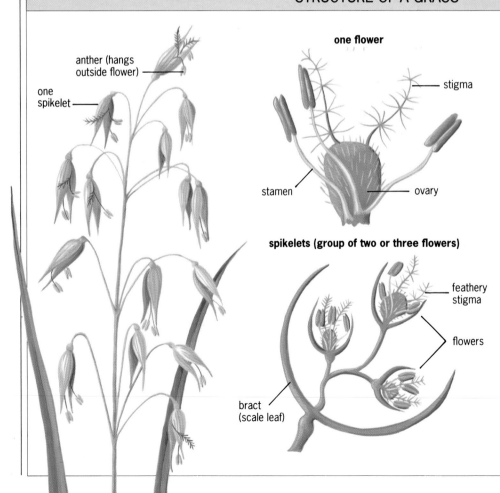

one flower

anther (hangs outside flower)

one spikelet

stigma

stamen

ovary

spikelets (group of two or three flowers)

feathery stigma

flowers

bract (scale leaf)

Above ground tall, thin shoots produce many tiny green flower spikes. The stem is divided into sections by nodes (joints) with a leaf attached at each node. Above the node the leaf is wrapped around the stem to form a sheath which partly covers the next section of stem. The rest of the leaf is free and forms a long, thin blade with parallel veins.

Grass flowers have no petals, because they are wind pollinated and do not need to attract insects. Instead they have green leaf-like scales to protect the flower parts. Each flower spikelet has a pair of outer scales enclosing one or more florets. Each floret has a pair of scales enclosing three stamens and an ovary with two feathery stigmas. Inside the ovary is an ovule which will later become the grain. The anthers are on long, fine stalks to hang outside the flower and release the pollen from the anthers. Pollination is by wind with the breeze carrying the pollen from the anthers to the feathery stigmas.

Numerous fine roots spread out to anchor the grass plant in the soil. Most are shallow-rooting, but some like marram grass, found on dry sand dunes, grow deep down into the ground. The roots of this sharp-leaved tussocky grass help to bind the sand grains together and stop the dunes moving.

produces smaller, more starchy grains. Maize contains fat as well as starch, and this is often extracted before the grains are ground into flour. It is used to make corn oil.

Wheat is grown all over the world but it grows best in temperate areas. It needs moist cool days to start with, then dry sunny days for ripening and harvesting. Strong wheat, with a high protein content, is grown in North America and the Ukraine. It is good for making bread. Durum wheat is a special kind of strong wheat which is used to make semolina, couscous and pasta. Weak wheat, with a lower protein content, is grown in Europe.

Rice grows best in the warmer parts of the world. It is a very important cereal in Asia because farmers can raise two and in some places three crops a year. Over half the world's population eats rice as a staple food. In Bangladesh, Indonesia, India, Nepal and parts of China some people eat hardly anything else. Most rice is grown in flooded fields called paddies, but upland rice grows like any other cereal.

Oats can grow in colder climates than wheat, rice or maize. Only the husk is removed in the milling, so oatmeal retains most of the fibre and all the nutrients of the grain. In northern Europe, ground or flaked oats are used to make porridge and oatcakes.

Barley is another cereal which likes a cooler climate. In some northern countries whole grain barley is used instead of potatoes or rice. Polished or pearl barley is used in soup. Most barley, however, is either malted to use in making beer or whisky, or is fed to cattle.

Rye also grows in colder climates where many other cereals will not survive. It is grown in Scandinavia, northern Germany and the Russia. Rye can be used in much the same way as wheat. Rye flour is usually whole grain and produces a darker and heavier bread than wheat.

Unusual grasses

Bamboo has woody stems, unlike other grasses, and may grow up to 40 m (130 ft) in height. Its stems provide an ideal building material and the leaves can be used for thatching; smaller stems make good fishing rods and garden stakes. Extract from the leaves of lemon grass is used to perfume soap and flavour curries. Pampas grass, an attractive perennial, produces feathery flower spikes and forms the centrepiece of many gardens.

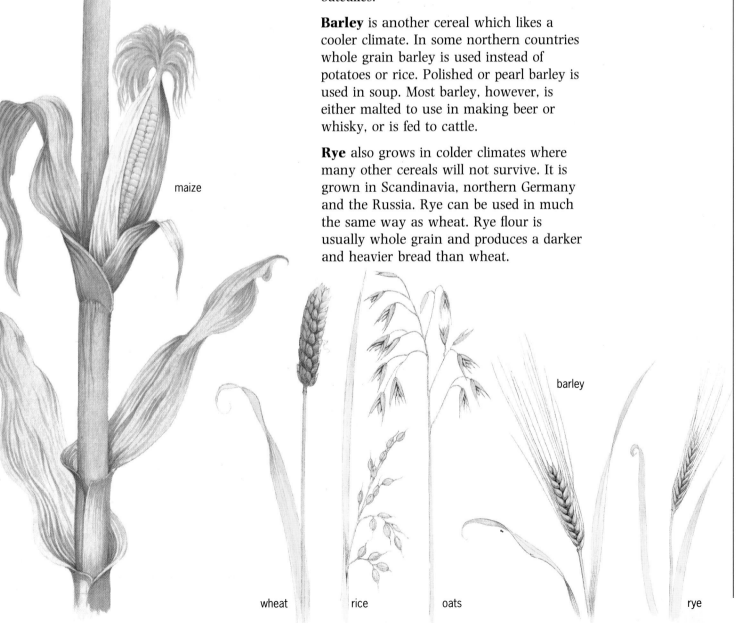

maize

wheat   rice   oats   barley   rye

Flowers

The biggest flower in the world is Rafflesia. It grows up to 1 m across and is produced by a parasitic plant which lives on the roots of lianas in the tropical rainforests of south-east Asia. It flowers once every ten years.

Some flowers are used as spices. Saffron comes from a Greek crocus. It has to be hand-picked and up to a quarter of a million flowers are needed to make one pound of this spice. It is the most expensive spice grown. Cloves are the dried flower buds of a tropical tree from Indonesia.

Flower buds such as those of cauliflower, calabrese, broccoli and globe artichokes are eaten as vegetables.

The flowers of hops are put into beer to give it a bitter flavour.

▶A flower contains a plant's reproductive organs. The male parts are called stamens and they produce pollen. The female parts are called carpels, and after fertilization they produce fruits and seeds.

Flowers contain a plant's reproductive organs. They produce fruits and seeds which give rise to the next generation of plants. Not all plants have flowers with brightly coloured and scented petals. Grasses have no petals, and some trees have petals so small you hardly notice them. Flower parts are arranged in rings on the end of a flower stalk. These parts come in many shapes and sizes, but they all have the same functions.

Parts of a flower

Sepals form the outermost ring of a flower. They are often green and look like small leaves. They cover and protect the flower at the bud stage of growth, and when the flower opens they usually bend back close to the stem.

Petals can be coloured and scented, with a tiny cup at the base called a nectary which produces sugary nectar. Petals like this attract insects which, when they come to collect nectar, transfer pollen from flower to flower. The majority of flowers have petals.

Stamens are a flower's male sex organs. Each consists of a stalk supporting a pair of anthers. An anther is a sausage-shaped bag containing pollen grains. Pollen grains contain the plant's male sex cells. Anthers open by splitting along their length and the two sides curl back to expose the pollen.

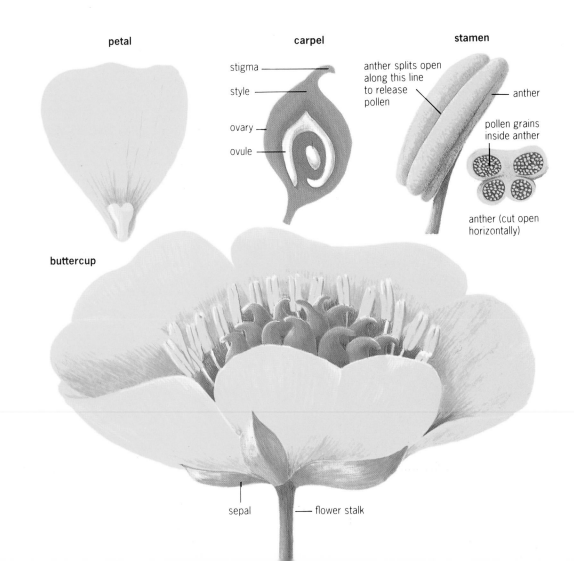

petal

carpel

stamen

stigma

style

ovary

ovule

anther splits open along this line to release pollen

anther

pollen grains inside anther

anther (cut open horizontally)

buttercup

sepal   flower stalk

POLLINATION AND FERTILIZATION

Most flowers have developed ways to ensure that pollen from one flower is carried to the stigma of another flower of the same kind. This is called cross-pollination. There are two main ways this takes place: by insects and by wind.

Insect pollination occurs because insects are attracted to a flower by its colour, smell, nectar and sometimes its pollen. White or cream flowers (such as honeysuckle and night-scented stocks) are pollinated by night-flying moths, which are also attracted by strong perfumes. Petals form a landing platform and many have special markings, called honey guides, to show the insect where the nectar is to be found. Some honey guides are invisible to us but can be seen when photographed in ultraviolet light, which insects' eyes can see. While the insect is searching for nectar, pollen grains cling to its body. These stick to the stigma of the next flower the insect visits.

Wind pollinated flowers need to be in a position to catch the breeze. Some, like grass flowers, grow above other plants on long stems. Others, like catkins, hang below the leaves or grow before leaf buds open. Pollen grains are small and light to float on the slightest breeze. They are produced from anthers dangling on long stalks, in huge quantities, because each grain has a very slight chance of reaching a stigma. Spreading, feathery stigmas act like nets to catch pollen drifting past.

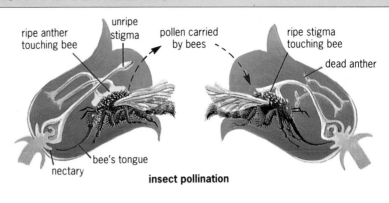

ripe anther touching bee · unripe stigma · pollen carried by bees · ripe stigma touching bee · dead anther · nectary · bee's tongue

insect pollination

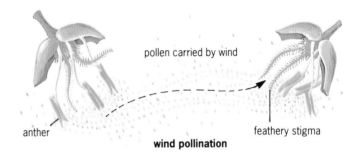

pollen carried by wind · anther · feathery stigma

wind pollination

Once a pollen grain sticks to a stigma of the same kind of flower it grows a tube down the style into an ovule in the ovary. The nucleus of a sex cell in the pollen grain moves down this tube and joins a nucleus in the ovule. This is called fertilization and starts the ovule developing into a seed, and the ovary into a fruit.

▲ Pollination is the transfer of pollen from the anthers of one flower to the stigmas in another flower of the same kind. This can be done by insects or the wind.

Carpels are a flower's female sex organs. Each has a swollen base, called the ovary, containing one or more ovules. These contain the plant's female sex cells. The top of a carpel forms a style, which ends in a pointed or flattened area called the stigma. Pollination is the transfer of pollen from anthers to stigmas. After pollination the ovary becomes a fruit and the ovules inside become seeds.

Arrangement of flowers

Many plants have one flower on the end of a stalk, but some have flowers arranged in groups. The simplest arrangement is a spike with the oldest flower at the bottom and the youngest bud at the top. Umbrella-like arrangements, called umbels, have

flower stalks of equal length at the end of a stem so the flowers form a flat head. Sunflowers, dandelions and thistles have 'flowers' made up of many tiny flowers called florets. Some florets are short tubes, like those at the centre of a sunflower. Others have strap-like petals like those at the edge of a sunflower.

▼ The simplest arrangement of flowers on a stem is one flower on the end of a stalk. But flowers are also arranged in other ways. The daisy type looks like one flower but is actually made up of many tiny flowers (florets).

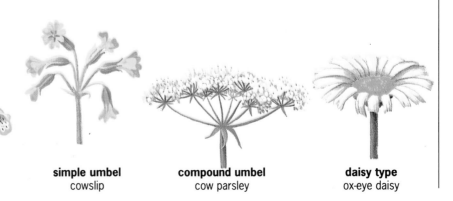

spike
foxglove

simple umbel
cowslip

compound umbel
cow parsley

daisy type
ox-eye daisy

Fruit

When we think of fruit we tend to think of apples, oranges and pears and the other fruits we eat. But 'fruit' is also used to describe the special part of a flowering plant in which seeds develop. Some fruits have a succulent flesh to attract animals which will then spread the seeds after eating the fruit. Others grow wings or hairy para-chutes to help them float when carried away by the wind. Each fruit has developed a successful way to spread its seeds and make sure the plant survives.

Pollination and fertilization are described in the article called Flowers.

Development of a fruit

Seeds developing in a fruit produce a special chemical called a 'growth hormone'. This causes the ovary to grow into a fruit. You can watch this development in the growth of a tomato. After pollination and fertili-zation the flower petals wither and drop off and the ovary swells into a round green fruit. A tiny brown point on the surface of the fruit opposite the stalk marks the

position of the style. If you cut through a tomato and look at one half you will see that each seed is attached to a swollen central part called the placenta. When the

◄ Plums have a fleshy outer layer surrounding a woody 'stone'. Inside is the kernel, the seed of the plum. This type of fruit is called a drupe. Peaches and apricots are also drupes.

◄ A blackberry is a collection of tiny drupes forming a compound fruit. Raspberries and loganberries are similar.

◄ In false fruits the fleshy part is not formed from the ovary wall. In apples and pears, for instance, the stalk swells out around the ovary to form the fruit.

◄ Bananas and some grapes have been bred to produce fruit without seeds. As no seeds are produced, new plants can only be obtained by taking cuttings of the parent plant.

◄ Some fruits, like the fruit of the cuckoopint, 'lords and ladies', are poisonous. Fruits that are poisonous to people are not necessarily poisonous to other animals, which help to spread the seeds by eating the fruit.

▼ Tomato developing from fertilized flower.

tomato has grown to full size it ripens by changing colour from green to red and developing a sweet flavour. It is now ready to spread its seeds.

Dispersal of soft fruits

Many soft fruits are eaten by animals, especially birds. The seeds inside the fruit pass through the animal's gut without being digested and fall to the ground in the animal's droppings. The seeds are now ready to grow surrounded by suitable fertilizer! The same happens when we eat a tomato, which is why there are always tomato plants at sewage farms. Some fruits, such as those of the parasitic plant mistletoe, are very sticky. The seeds cling to birds' beaks, and are then wiped off into cracks in the bark when the birds clean their beaks. The seed germinates and a new mistletoe plant grows from the crack in the bark.

Dispersal of dry fruits

Some fruits use wind to carry them away from the parent plant. Sycamore, field maple and ash all have winged fruits called keys. In dandelion and thistle, parachutes of hairs support the fruits in the wind. Poppies and orchids produce tiny, lightweight seeds which are scattered when the fruits sway in the breeze.

Plants growing near water, like the coconut palm, may use it to carry their fruits. In waterlilies each seed has its own float to support it when carried away by the current. Other fruits like balsam explode, scattering their seeds great distances. On a hot day you may hear the popping of the dry pods on broom as they suddenly twist open and fling out their seeds.

Animals spread fruits when they collect them for their food stores. Squirrels may hide hazelnuts underground, and if they are forgotten they are already planted for the next growing season. Other fruits, like cleavers, have hooks which catch in the fur of a passing animal. These are spread when the animal grooms itself and tosses away the fur ball around the fruit.

▲ Yellow-necked mouse with rosehip. The mouse eats the rosehip but it is unable to digest its seeds. These will pass unharmed through the mouse's gut, to germinate in the mouse's droppings.

NUTS AND SEEDS

Seeds

Seeds are produced by flowering plants and conifers. Each one is able to grow into a new plant given the right conditions. Seeds of flowering plants develop inside fruits while those of conifers develop inside cones. Seeds contain a partly developed plant complete with tiny root, leaves and a supply of food. These are wrapped in a protective seed coat called a testa. Seeds enable plants to survive periods like winter or a dry season when normal growth is impossible.

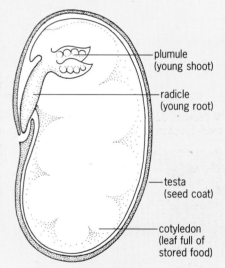

plumule (young shoot)

radicle (young root)

testa (seed coat)

cotyledon (leaf full of stored food)

coconut

milk

flesh (stored food)

embryo (young plant)

husk (fibres)

Nuts

Nuts are fruits or seeds with a tough or woody outer skin forming the shell. Inside this is the kernel, which is the part of the nut you can eat. The kernel is actually a young plant. It has cotyledons that contain the stored food that it needs to grow. These are also a good food source for nut-eating animals such as squirrels, as most nuts are rich in protein and fat. Animals which feed on nuts must have strong teeth to gnaw through the protective shell. Some chimpanzees use bits of wood or a rock as a hammer to crack open nuts.

Leaves

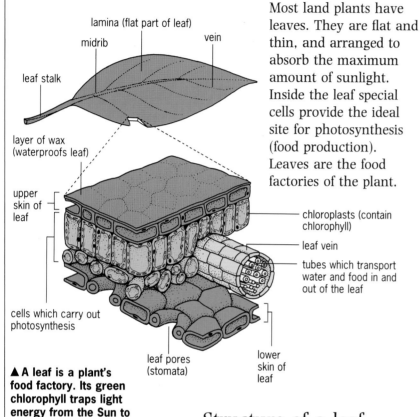

lamina (flat part of leaf)

midrib

vein

leaf stalk

layer of wax
(waterproofs leaf)

upper
skin of
leaf

cells which carry out
photosynthesis

chloroplasts (contain
chlorophyll)

leaf vein

tubes which transport
water and food in and
out of the leaf

leaf pores
(stomata)

lower
skin of
leaf

▲ A leaf is a plant's
food factory. Its green
chlorophyll traps light
energy from the Sun to
change carbon dioxide
and water into sugar.
The veins supply the
leaf with water and
transport sugar as fast
as it is made away from
the leaf to other parts
of the plant.

Most land plants have
leaves. They are flat and
thin, and arranged to
absorb the maximum
amount of sunlight.
Inside the leaf special
cells provide the ideal
site for photosynthesis
(food production).
Leaves are the food
factories of the plant.

Structure of a leaf

Each leaf consists of a broad, flat blade
supported by a central midrib and
branching veins. The veins form a network
of tiny tubes connecting all parts of the
plant. A leaf stalk, the petiole, attaches the

leaf to the stem. Among dead leaves in the
spring you may find 'leaf skeletons'. These
are the remains of the veins when the rest
of the leaf has rotted. The leaf blade is like a
sandwich. Upper and lower layers hold a
green 'filling' of cells containing the green
pigment chlorophyll.

How leaves work

Cells in the middle of a leaf contain chloroplasts which are tiny bags of chlorophyll.
Chlorophyll uses the Sun's light energy to
make food from water and carbon dioxide.
This process is called photosynthesis. The
food is carried in the veins as liquid sugars
to growth or storage areas. Water enters the
cells from the veins after the roots have
absorbed it from the soil. Some water is lost
by evaporation from stomata (pores) on the
leaf underside. If there is not enough water
the leaves wilt, only recovering if the plant
is watered. The movement of water through
a plant is called the transpiration stream.

As leaves on deciduous trees die at the end
of summer the green chlorophyll pigment
changes into yellow, red and brown. A cork
layer grows across the base of the leaf stalk
cutting off the leaf's water supply. Without
water the leaf shrivels, dies and falls off.

LEAF SHAPES

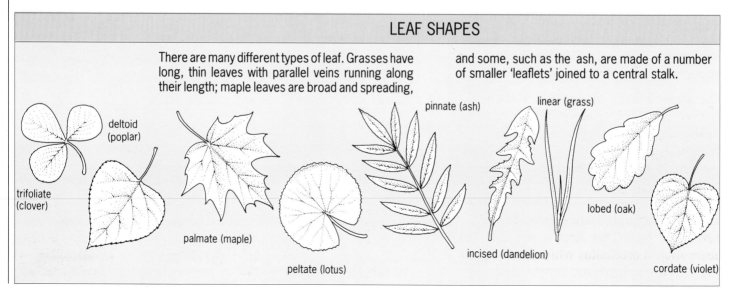

There are many different types of leaf. Grasses have
long, thin leaves with parallel veins running along
their length; maple leaves are broad and spreading,

and some, such as the ash, are made of a number
of smaller 'leaflets' joined to a central stalk.

deltoid
(poplar)

trifoliate
(clover)

palmate (maple)

peltate (lotus)

pinnate (ash)

incised (dandelion)

linear (grass)

lobed (oak)

cordate (violet)

Flowerless plants

The first plants to evolve did not have flowers. Some of these plants survive today.

Algae

Algae are the simplest plants. Nearly all grow in water and the best-known are seaweeds. Some grow in moist places on land, like the green scum on damp ground and the powdery green layer on the bark of some trees. Some live inside corals and other water animals, and others live with fungi to form a group called lichens. Algae vary in size from microscopic plants which have only one cell to giant sea kelps, brown seaweeds which can grow up to 45 m (150 ft) long.

Algae are divided into groups by colour. Blue-green algae can be microscopic or occur in clumps or long threads. They can live in freezing Antarctic lakes, near boiling hot springs and even on bare rock. Green algae live mainly in fresh water and include blanket weed, which can cover ponds and streams which are polluted with fertilizer washed out of the soil by rain. Brown and red algae include the seaweeds found on most rocky shores.

Ferns

Ferns are usually found in damp places. Their leaves grow from an underground stem and are often arranged in a circle, uncoiling like a spring as they develop.

The underside of a mature fern leaf often has brown, powdery areas. These are clusters of little sacs (sporangia) which contain tiny reproductive spores. As a spore sac dries it suddenly splits open, flinging spores in all directions. They are light enough to be carried by the wind. If they land in a damp place they grow, but not into a new fern. They form a tiny thin, flat, heart-shaped prothallus which looks like a leaf. It has the fern's sex organs on its

◀ The brown patches on the underside of this fern leaf are the sporangia which produce the spores.

underside. When the ground is damp, male sex organs release swimming sperms which fertilize a female egg cell, and it is this which grows into a new fern plant.

Mosses

Moss plants grow together in groups, sometimes forming green velvety cushions or spreading mats. It is very rare to find single plants. In woods mosses may form a green carpet over the damp soil, covering rotten logs and growing up the bark at the base of tree trunks. The best time to see mosses is in early spring when they are not hidden by other plants.

▼ Almost all of the 7,000 species of seaweeds are algae. They are divided into groups of red, brown and green algae.

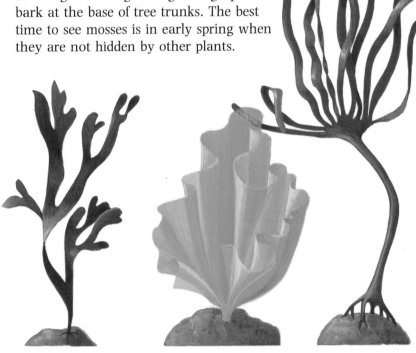

Evolution

When the Earth was first formed, there was no life at all. The surface of the Earth was very hot then, and nothing could have lived. It took about 1,000 million years for the Earth to become suitable for life. It is very hard to imagine how life could arise from non-living things. For years, biologists could not understand how the very complicated plants and animals, including ourselves, could have come from simple chemicals.

However, some very simple microscopic forms of life have been discovered and these seem to be partly like living things and partly like chemicals which are not alive.

For instance, viruses can reproduce but are so simple that they can be made into crystals like other chemicals.

Scientists think that life arose from chemicals that entered the atmosphere from volcanoes, thousands of millions of years ago. Geologists can tell from ancient rocks that these chemicals included hydrogen, methane, ammonia, and water, but no oxygen. Experiments have shown that these chemicals will form into molecules called amino acids quite easily.

Amino acids are the building blocks of proteins, and proteins are the main substances of living things. Experiments in laboratories have suggested that lightning and radiation from the Sun triggered the formation of amino acids. These dissolved in the oceans where, over millions of years, they formed proteins and then simple cells.

These simple cells were like small bags of protein with an outer membrane which could take in other chemicals (feed) and divide to form new cells (reproduce). The oldest fossils that have been discovered are 3,500 million years old. They support these ideas.

After many hundreds of years, the cells gradually changed and became bigger. They had a special structure called a nucleus, which controlled the whole cell. Simple creatures made up from several cells appeared about 850 million years ago. At first these were just strings of cells, like chains of beads.

It took many millions of years for these strings of cells to evolve into recognizable animals and plants. The first true land plants lived about 410 million years ago. Bony fish appeared around 400 million years ago, and it was only about 65 million years ago that the first mammals lived.

DARWIN'S THEORY OF EVOLUTION

▲ While on the Galapagos Islands, Darwin observed several species of finch, each with a different shape of bill to suit its method of feeding.

As a young man Charles Darwin (1809–1882) went as the naturalist on the five-year expedition of the naval survey ship HMS *Beagle*. Darwin was able to see and study many different animals and plants on his journey, but the most important part of the voyage was the few weeks the *Beagle* spent in the Galapagos Islands. Here Darwin found plants and animals that are found nowhere else. Each island had its own sort of tortoise and its own sorts of finch. They were similar but different. Why should this be Darwin wondered?

Darwin suggested that those living things most likely to survive and reproduce are those most suited to their environments. All living things produce large numbers of young, yet in spite of this the numbers of living things stay much the same. Some living things must have a better chance of breeding. If, every now and again, an animal was born with some feature which gave it an advantage, it would survive to breed, and so would its offspring that were like it. The feature would become more common. Darwin called this natural selection. Darwin published his ideas in 1879 in his book *Origin of Species*. It caused an uproar at the time, but now most people accept Darwin's theory of evolution.

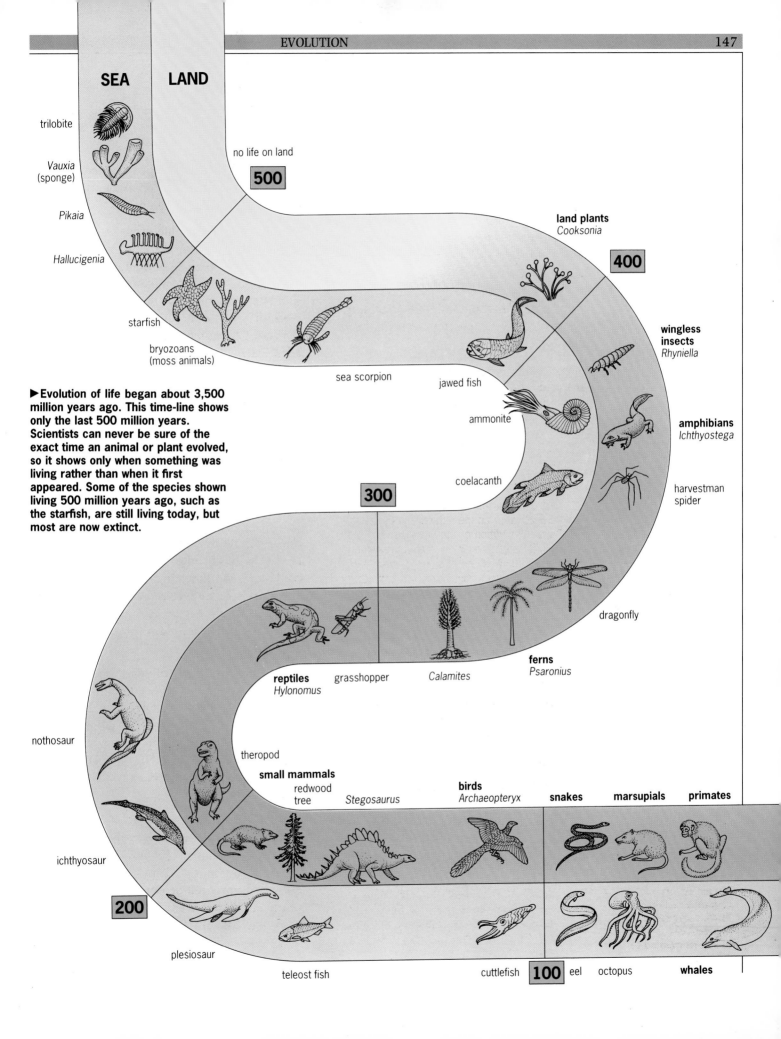

SEA   LAND

trilobite

Vauxia
(sponge)

Pikaia

Hallucigenia

no life on land

500

starfish

bryozoans
(moss animals)

sea scorpion

jawed fish

land plants
Cooksonia

400

wingless
insects
Rhyniella

ammonite

amphibians
Ichthyostega

coelacanth

harvestman
spider

►Evolution of life began about 3,500
million years ago. This time-line shows
only the last 500 million years.
Scientists can never be sure of the
exact time an animal or plant evolved,
so it shows only when something was
living rather than when it first
appeared. Some of the species shown
living 500 million years ago, such as
the starfish, are still living today, but
most are now extinct.

300

dragonfly

reptiles
Hylonomus

grasshopper

Calamites

ferns
Psaronius

nothosaur

theropod

small mammals
redwood
tree   *Stegosaurus*

birds
Archaeopteryx   **snakes**   **marsupials**   **primates**

ichthyosaur

200

plesiosaur

teleost fish

cuttlefish **100** eel octopus   **whales**

Evolution of people

All the people living in the world today belong to a species of mammal called *Homo sapiens*. This name means 'wise man' in Latin, and is used because of the very large brain and intelligence of modern human beings compared to their predecessors or to other animals.

Nearest living relatives

Scientists noticed long ago that the living animals which are most like humans are the great apes. Like humans, the apes have large brains and long arms with powerful hands for picking things up. Unlike most other species of primate, the great apes do not have tails.

Methods developed in the last 20 years or so have allowed us to study the protein molecules and the DNA molecules in the cells of animals. These molecules change slowly as time passes and the animals evolve. So we can tell which animals are related to which by how similar these molecules are. In this way, scientists now know that chimpanzees are the nearest living relatives of modern humans. The gorilla is nearly as close. Also, these molecules tell us that the animals which

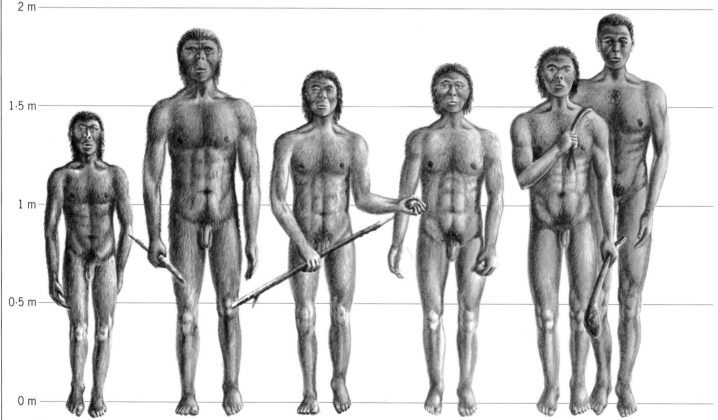

Australopithecus afarensis were about 1·5 m tall. They were able to walk upright but they did have longer arms and shorter legs than humans. They lived between 3 and 4 million years ago

Australopithecus robustus were about 1·75 m tall and weighed about 60 kg. They lived between one and 2·2 million years ago and, probably lived on fruit, roots, and leaves.

Homo habilis lived between 0·9 and 2·1 million years ago. They were about 1·6 tall and 40 kg in weight. They looked less like apes, had larger brains and probably used tools.

Homo erectus lived between 0·3 and 1·6 million years ago and had even larger brains than *Homo habilis*. They made tools, hunted meat, used fire and had home bases.

Neanderthals lived between 30 and 150 thousand years ago. They hunted, made tools, and wore clothes as well. Their skeletons were heavier than those of modern people.

A more modern kind of *Homo sapiens* lived at the same time as the Neanderthals and eventually replaced them.

eventually evolved into humans separated from the ancestors of the great apes about 5 million years ago.

Fossils

Fossilized bones have been dug up from many parts of the world, and these tell us about the evolution of humans. The very earliest kinds of fossils that are believed to be from the ancestors of humans have been found in Africa and are about 3 to 4 million years old. These ancestors are called *Australopithecus*.

Several slightly different kinds of *Australopithecus* lived in Africa until about 1 million years ago. But fossils of a new and more human-like creature have been found in rocks nearly 2 million years old, in the Olduvai Gorge in Tanzania. These have bigger brains than *Australopithecus*, and we know they also made simple stone tools. Scientists believe that they evolved from *Australopithecus*. They are named *Homo habilis*, which means 'handy man'. They were more like modern humans than *Australopithecus*.

Another kind of fossil that is even more like modern humans has been found. This is about 1·6 million years old. The species recorded in this fossil had a yet bigger brain than *Homo habilis*, and was able to make better tools such as hand axes, and also to make fires. It is called *Homo erectus*, which means 'upright person', and it first appeared in Africa. Fossils of *Homo erectus* have also been found in many other places in the world: in Europe, China, the Middle East and Java. These creatures still had brains that were a little smaller than modern human brains. They were also shorter and had thick skull bones.

We think that the modern kind of human beings evolved from *Homo erectus*.

The Neanderthal people

The remains of a human skeleton were discovered in the Neander Valley in West Germany in 1856. It was a member of *Homo sapiens*, but was a bit shorter and stockier than most modern people and had a more sloping forehead. Similar fossils have since been found in many parts of Europe. They are called the Neanderthals. They lived from about 150,000 years ago until about 30,000 years ago. We know from the objects found with them that they had several kinds of tools such as scrapers and flint knives. They also buried their dead. They seem to have been well able to live during the ice ages. Nobody knows why they gradually died out. Perhaps they were driven out by more modern people.

Prehistoric people

As Neanderthals disappeared, a more modern kind of *Homo sapiens* was spreading. They were taller and more slender, but did not have larger brains. By about 10,000 years ago these modern people lived almost everywhere.

▲ The skull of the Neanderthal (left) is larger than the skull of the Cro-Magnon, a more modern kind of *Homo sapiens* living at the same time. Some people believe this is because Neanderthals had larger brains.

One of the best examples of *Australopithecus* is a skeleton that the discoverers nicknamed 'Lucy'. It was found in Ethiopia in 1974. 'Lucy' was quite a lot smaller than modern humans, and had a much smaller brain. But she had teeth that are like those of modern humans and she could walk upright. In fact there is a famous set of fossilized footprints in Tanzania that shows how *Australopithecus* must have walked upright as we do today.

Dinosaurs

Long dinosaur
Diplodocus 27 m

Tall dinosaur
Brachiosaurus 12 m

Small dinosaur
Compsognathus
75–91 cm; 3 kg

Large dinosaur
Ultrasaurus
Length 20 m
Weight 130 tonnes

Dinosaurs are among the most varied and amazing animals that have ever lived on Earth. They were a type of reptile, related to the crocodiles and also the birds. Some, like *Compsognathus*, were as small as a chicken. Others, like *Apatosaurus*, were larger than ten elephants. Over a thousand species of dinosaurs are known to have existed. They flourished on Earth for about 160 million years. The first lived about 225 million years ago, and the last ones lived about 65 million years ago.

Strange giant bones

Dinosaurs are known from their fossils, the remains of their bones preserved in the rocks. The first fossil of a dinosaur that was recorded came from a stone quarry near Oxford. The end of a giant thigh-bone was brought to Robert Plot, the Professor of Chemistry at Oxford University, in 1677. Plot had no idea that it came from a giant extinct reptile. More giant bones were found in the next century, but no one had any idea what they were.

In the 1820s more bones were found near Oxford and the Professor of Geology studied them. These bones included a jaw with long, sharp teeth, each the size of a steak knife. He realized that these came from a giant extinct reptile, and he gave it a name: *Megalosaurus*, meaning 'giant lizard'. This was the first dinosaur to be named.

The second species of dinosaur given a name was *Iguanodon* (iguana tooth). The name was invented by Gideon Mantell, who thought it was a giant lizard, since the fossil teeth were like those of a modern iguana lizard, only dozens of times bigger.

More fossils were found and the English scientist Sir Richard Owen showed that they belonged to a group of large reptiles that had lived a very long time ago, and which were quite unlike any of the living reptiles. He invented the name dinosaurs, from Greek words meaning 'terrible lizards'.

RECONSTRUCTION

From dinosaur bones we can build up a picture of what the dinosaur may have looked like.

First the skeleton of the dinosaur is made up from the bones that have been found. Missing bones have to be made up with plaster or fibre-glass. The skeleton then tells us the general size and shape of the dinosaur, and how it stood.

Next, the size and the positions of the main muscles of the body are guessed at, as well as the likely outline of the belly. In this way, the overall shape that the body would have been can be worked out.

Finally the scientist must guess what the scales and the skin were like when the animal was alive. He or she can also imagine what colour it was, and perhaps what kind of expression it had on its face.

Main groups of dinosaurs

The first dinosaurs were fairly small two-legged creatures which fed on insects and lizards. They had long tails, and short arms which could be used to grasp things. Sometime in the Triassic period of Earth's history, about 200 million years ago, the dinosaurs evolved into two main branches. These can be told apart by the way their hip-bones are arranged. Those with lizard-like hips are called Saurischia; and those with bird-like hips, Ornithischia.

The lizard-hipped Saurischia split into two lines in the Late Triassic period. The first of these, the Theropoda (beast feet), walked on two legs and ate meat. The chicken-sized *Compsognathus* and the fearsome 15 m (50 ft) long *Tyrannosaurus* belonged to this group. The other lizard-hipped line, the Sauropodomorpha (reptile feet), were plant eaters. Some of the species in this group, such as *Diplodocus* and *Apatosaurus*, had

Archaeopteryx

One of the most famous fossils is *Archaeopteryx*, the earliest known fossil of a bird. This fossil is very well known because it is a 'missing link' between the dinosaurs and the birds as we know them today. The first fossil of *Archaeopteryx* was found in Germany in 1861. This showed an almost complete skeleton of a small animal with very slender bones. It was about the size of a pigeon, and had teeth, a long tail, and feathers.

▲ *Archaeopteryx* was quite similar to small dinosaurs like *Compsognathus*, except that it had feathers.

▼ This is a family tree to show how the dinosaurs evolved over millions of years.

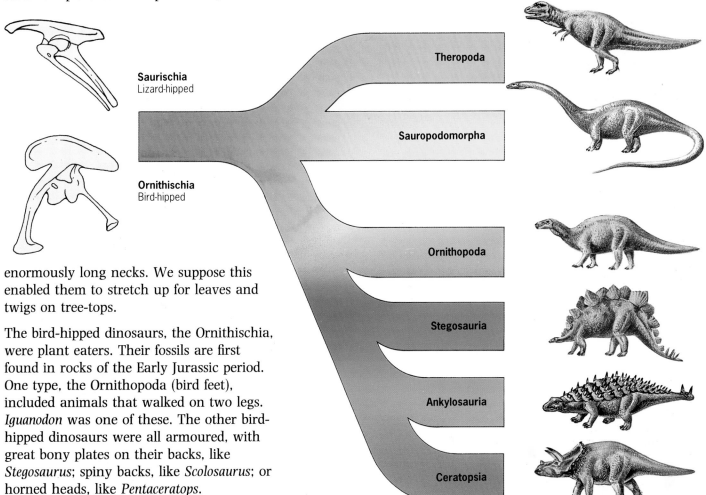

Saurischia
Lizard-hipped

Ornithischia
Bird-hipped

Theropoda

Sauropodomorpha

Ornithopoda

Stegosauria

Ankylosauria

Ceratopsia

enormously long necks. We suppose this enabled them to stretch up for leaves and twigs on tree-tops.

The bird-hipped dinosaurs, the Ornithischia, were plant eaters. Their fossils are first found in rocks of the Early Jurassic period. One type, the Ornithopoda (bird feet), included animals that walked on two legs. *Iguanodon* was one of these. The other bird-hipped dinosaurs were all armoured, with great bony plates on their backs, like *Stegosaurus*; spiny backs, like *Scolosaurus*; or horned heads, like *Pentaceratops*.

Dinosaur diets

Most dinosaurs fed on plants. Some of the giant sauropodomorphs probably ate the leaves of the tops of trees, using their long necks. They must have been feeding all day, because they were so large, up to 100 tonnes in weight, and because of the relatively small size of their heads. Some of the ornithopods were able to eat very tough plants like reeds and ferns. This is shown by their unusual teeth, which were arranged in many rows. Some of them had as many as 2,000 teeth in operation at any time! The theropods were all meat eaters. The small theropods must have fed on lizards and other small animals, but the larger ones must have preyed on the plant-eating dinosaurs.

▲ **Reconstruction of reptiles in their natural habitat in the late Triassic period, about 220 million years ago. Numbers 2 and 3 are dinosaurs.**

1 *Kuehneosaurus*
2 *Plateosaurus*
3 *Coelophysis*

▶ **Some of the dinosaurs and plants which lived 150 million years ago (Jurassic period) in America.**

1 *Diplodocus*
2 *Stegosaurus*
3 *Camarasaurus*
4 *Allosaurus*
5 *Compsognathus*

Warm-blooded or cold?

Scientists do not know whether dinosaurs were warm-blooded or cold-blooded. A cold-blooded animal like a lizard needs heat from the Sun to keep warm. It does not always have cold blood and it does need to warm up to become active. Warm-blooded animals, such as birds and human beings, burn up food to keep their bodies at the same warm temperature all the time. Since the climate was warm, the dinosaurs would have had no problem in keeping warm during the day. The big dinosaurs could stay warm through the night because it would take a long time for their massive bodies to lose heat. Smaller dinosaurs may have warmed themselves by exercise. Scientists are still arguing about these questions.

The end of the dinosaurs

No one knows why the dinosaurs disappeared. As far as we can tell, they lived right to the end of the Cretaceous period, 65 million years ago, and then disappeared quite suddenly. Scientists do not know exactly how long the disappearance took. It could have happened in one day, or it might have taken as much as a million years.

Many other living things disappeared at about the same time. In the sea, the ammonites and belemnites disappeared, as well as the last of the great sea reptiles: the plesiosaurs, and the mosasaurs.

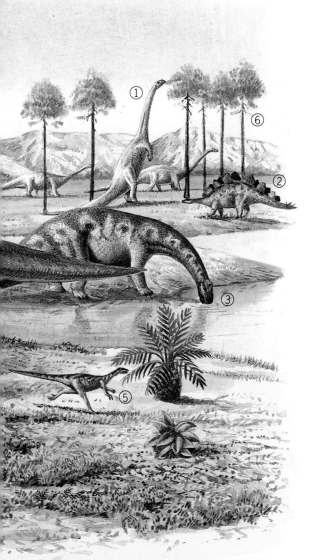

So what did happen?

There are two main theories now which explain the disappearance of the dinosaurs. One is that climates were changing and becoming cooler everywhere. The dinosaurs and many other animals and plants were not able to adapt enough to the new colder conditions. After a time, they just died off.

The other theory is that the Earth was hit by a giant meteorite. This exploded on the surface of the Earth and sent up a huge cloud of dust which spread around the Earth and blacked out the Sun. This caused the Earth to freeze up for a while. Plants and animals died off everywhere, and only those which could withstand the cold were able to survive and then recolonize the Earth a year or so later. No one can decide which of these theories is correct.

▲ These dinosaurs (and the pterodactyl) lived on land that is now Canada about 75 million years ago in the late Cretaceous period.

1 *Pterodactylus*
2 *Tyrannosaurus*
3 *Parasaurolophus*
4 *Struthiomimus*

Prehistoric animals

Tens of thousands of years ago, giant woolly mammoths and rhinoceroses lived in Europe and mastodons lived in North America. These prehistoric animals lived at the same time as early humans, but long before people began to write down the story of human history. This is why they are called *prehistoric* animals.

Prehistoric animals also include such creatures as the dinosaurs, but these were much more ancient and lived long before humans appeared on the Earth.

Baluchitherium

The first mammals

Mammals arose during the age of the dinosaurs, about 210 million years ago. These early forms were generally small and probably looked rather like shrews. They were agile little animals with many small, pointed teeth. It is thought that most of them fed on insects. During the rest of the dinosaur age, the mammals did not become very important. After their first 140 million years of evolution, the largest one was still only cat-sized. No one could ever have guessed that the small, shy, hairy animals, which scuttled in and out of the undergrowth, would eventually rule the Earth.

When the dinosaurs died out 65 million years ago, the mammals had a chance to evolve. Over the next 10 million years, the mouse-

American mastodon

Procoptodon goliah

Diprotodon optatum

sized and cat-sized mammals gave rise to all of the major groups of mammals alive today: horses, dogs and cats, cattle and deer, monkeys and apes, bats, whales, anteaters, kangaroos, and many more.

Giant mammals

Once the mammals had become established, some remarkable giant forms arose. One strange early group was the brontotheres (thunder mammals), which had a massive forked horn on their snouts, shaped rather like a catapult. The brontotheres reached a height of 2 m (6·5 ft) at the shoulder, about the size of a half-grown elephant, but they died out, leaving no descendants.

The rhinoceroses may have taken over from these two groups to some extent. Thirty million years ago, there were dozens of species of rhinoceros living in North America, in particular. Some of these were small fast-running animals which looked like a cross between a small rhino and a horse. Others were very large: *Baluchitherium* from central Asia reached the enormous height of 5 m (17 ft) at the shoulder, and it probably weighed eight times as much as the biggest rhino today.

Sabre-toothed cats

Some of the best-known prehistoric animals are the sabre-toothed cats which lived in many parts of the world during the last 25 million years. There were many different

species of sabre-tooths, and all of them had especially long canine teeth (the slightly pointed teeth that you have near the front of your mouth). In some sabre-tooths the canines were 15 cm (6 in) or more in length. They probably fed on the large plant-eating mammals and needed the extra-long teeth to pierce their thick hides. The last sabre-tooths died out only a few tens of thousands of years ago.

Prehistoric elephants

In the past elephants were quite common and varied. Some prehistoric elephants were no bigger than a pig, while others were half as big again as the biggest kind alive now. Some had no trunk; some had four tusks; others had tusks on the lower jaw shaped like shovels, or tiny tusks. The woolly mammoths of Europe and Asia and the mastodons of North America, lived from about 2 million years ago and died out as little as 10,000 years ago. This may have been because of changes in the climate at the end of the last ice age, or because early humans hunted them to death.

▲ This kind of sabre-toothed cat ranged over North and South America, and probably fed on mastodons and ground sloths.

◄ The extinction of the dinosaurs enabled mammals to flourish, and many giant forms evolved, such as the enormous Baluchitherium, a rhinoceros which stood 5 m high at the shoulder.

Shasta ground sloth

Glyptodont

Extinct animals

Carolina parakeet extinct 1918

quagga extinct 1883

aurochs extinct 1627

giant moa extinct about 1500

dodo extinct 1681

flightless ibis extinct about 1000

giant lemur extinct about AD 500

99 per cent of all the animal species that have ever lived are now extinct.

Most animal and plant species that have lived on Earth are now extinct. We know about them only from their fossils, unless the extinctions were recent.

Extinctions have occurred throughout Earth's history, but have increased in recent years. Hundreds of species are dying out every year.

Why it happens

Animals may become extinct in at least three ways.

1 They may evolve into another species, so they do not really die out, only change. Human beings are a good example: Neanderthal people are extinct, but we are not.

2 A species may become extinct because of changes in its habitat. Those animals with very limited diets are particularly at risk. The giant panda, which eats only bamboo,

is more likely to become extinct than the rat which eats most things.

The mammoths and woolly rhinos of Europe were adapted to the cold conditions of the ice age. As the ice age ended and the climate became warmer, they were unable to adapt, and this may have led to their extinction.

3 Mass extinction is when thousands of species die out all over the world at the same time. There may have been ten or more mass extinctions in the past 600 million years. Scientists want to learn why these extinctions occurred. Some think they were a result of gradual climate changes, lasting 1–5 million years. Others believe they were caused by meteor showers. As many as half of all living species may have been wiped out by great explosions, and as a result of dust clouds shutting out the sunlight. No one knows yet what really happened.

Index